*WILDERNESS PARISH*

# Wilderness Parish

## BY C. S. COOPER

Pacific Press Publishing Association

Mountain View, California

Omaha, Nebraska  •  Portland, Oregon

# DEDICATION

*To the faithful advent believers of the northland who have made these stories possible, and to my wife and two daughters who have cheerfully faced the ruggedness of our wilderness parish, this book is affectionately dedicated.*

# CONTENTS

# 1

## CALL TO ADVENTURE

THE jangle of the telephone broke my train of thought; shattered it, even. I've never been able to understand people who can sit calmly through half a dozen rings, then slowly go to the instrument and lift the receiver. A telephone call is intriguing. It may be only a bid for a chat with a neighbor, but it just might be a long-distance call from a faraway place. It might bring news of disaster, or it might bring a message capable of changing the whole course of life.

The instrument had not rung a second time before I was out of my chair. A hundred monotonous rehearsals of routine affairs had not dimmed my hope that *this* call might be an exciting one. It was, or I wouldn't be writing about it.

"Long distance is calling C. S. Cooper," said the impersonal voice of the operator.

"This *is* Mr. Cooper," I replied.

(1)

"Here is your party," said the operator, "go ahead, please."

"Hello! Brother Cooper?" queried a voice that sounded familiar.

"Yes, this is Cooper," I repeated as my mind sought through the past for identification of this voice.

"How are you, and how are the wife and the little girls?" continued the voice. Now it was coming back to me. In California where I had served my first years as a minister this man had been a neighboring pastor and a valued friend of mine.

"Elder Smithwick!" I exclaimed, as I tried to recall his present position and guess why he would be calling me. "We're all fine. I hardly expected a call from you. What have I done?"

"It's not what you've done," he replied with a chuckle; "it's what you're going to do. What would you think of going north into some pioneer territory—up around Lac la Hache and Prince George and Lamming Mills? We need someone who has good health and the spirit of adventure."

These names of settlements in British Columbia meant little to me. In fact, the call was so unexpected and I was so unfamiliar with the geography of Canada's most western province, that I was totally unprepared to make a decision on the basis of whether or not I would like to live in the district indicated. Perhaps it was better that way. Now all I knew was that there was a place in the northland where I was needed.

Early in my ministry I had decided that the Lord would lead the conference brethren in deciding where I should labor. So as soon as Elder Smithwick assured me that the invitation had been cleared through the proper channels, I told him that I would come.

Arrangements for moving were completed and the time

set for the transfer. The entire transaction was completed in less than ten minutes and I replaced the telephone receiver on its hook. Now I had time to think! Had I acted rashly? Where were those towns Elder Smithwick had said would be in my district? And what would Virginia, my wife, and our two girls, Kathleen and Carolynn, think about the change? Perhaps I should have taken a little time to think this proposition through before making my decision.

I obtained a road map of British Columbia from an oil company and gathered the family around to see where our new field of labor would be. A place called Cache Creek was to mark the sourthern boundary of our territory. This we spotted on the map 221 miles by road northeast of the port city of Vancouver. About 100 miles farther north was Lac la Hache, where a company of believers had recently been organized into a church. One hundred and six miles beyond Lac la Hache was the town of Quesnel where a small Sabbath school was meeting regularly. Still another eighty miles to the north was the city of Prince George, with a well-established church and church school. It was decided that we should make our home there so that the girls could have the privilege of attending that school.

One hundred and seventy miles southeast of Prince George is located Lamming Mills, a large lumber operation owned by Ernie and Oscar Lamming and manned by a crew of men of whom most were Seventh-day Adventists. From Prince George we traced the road leading still farther to the north, over the Canadian Rockies and on to Dawson Creek, where the Alcan Highway begins. Forty-nine miles up the Alcan and 304 miles north of Prince George is a settlement called Fort Saint John, which would mark the northern outpost of our district. In this vast area north of Prince George we would find no organized church, but there would be a number of Adventist families living in isolated small groups or alone.

The prospect was both challenging and overwhelming. Never before had I been confronted with a task that, because of its sheer physical dimensions, seemed so impossible. From Cache Creek to Fort Saint John is 600 miles by road, or about 400 air-line miles. Reaching out east and west of this road the district included a strip of sparsely settled bushland roughly 250 miles wide. Laying a ruler on the map, I calculated that I had said Yes to a hundred thousand square miles of Canadian wilderness.

A parish of one hundred thousand square miles! Superimpose it upon California and you would cover almost all of that state south of the city of Sacramento. Or take Maine, New Hampshire, Vermont, Massachusetts, Rhode Island, Connecticut, and most of New York, and you would have an area comparable in size. It sounded fantastic. Did the conference expect one man to serve it all? There was still time to back out. But, no. I had given my word, and with God's help I would do what I could to serve the people of British Columbia's northland. Happily, Virginia and the girls loyally concurred with this decision, and soon all hands were busy packing the family possessions.

Three weeks later our goods were loaded on a truck, and we were in our car headed for British Columbia—and adventure!

We had been asked to stop at the conference office in Mission City on our way into the north. This we did, and we found a modest modern building housing the headquarters of our work in British Columbia. The office staff gave us a warm, friendly welcome and we were ushered into a comfortable room, where we were greeted by the president, Elder R. A. Smithwick.

I presume that he felt obligated to soften the blow he expected us to receive when, fresh from city life, paved highways, and every modern convenience, we would find ourselves thrust into a district not yet emerged from the era of frontier days. At any rate, Elder Smithwick briefed us on conditions along what he called the "northline," and assured us that he would arrange our transfer to a more suitable place in the conference as soon as possible.

We drove east, early the next morning, along Highway No. 1 to the small town of Hope. Here the road turns abruptly north, crosses the Fraser River by bridge, and, within a short distance, leads into the narrow, precipitous confines of the Fraser River canyon. We found the great river squeezed into the bottom of a deep gorge where it boils and roars its fearsome way on toward the Pacific. The road—a miracle of pioneer engineering, at times down close to the river's edge, then up near the top of a sheer precipice; now blasted out of a perpendicular rock wall, then suspended over the raging current by a framework of huge wooden beams—somehow eventually traverses the seventy-one miles to Lytton, where the Thompson River adds its flow of water to the Fraser. Here the highway leaves the larger river and follows the Thompson upstream for forty-five miles through scenery barely less spectacular than that of the Fraser canyon.

Swinging away from the Thompson River, the highway next crosses a stretch of barren country quite desertlike in appearance. In the midst of this miniature desert we came to Cache Creek, a small community which exists almost entirely to serve travelers. The town consists of a few service stations, a grocery store, a café, and accommodations for overnight lodging.

We were now more keenly interested than ever in what

lay to the north, for from now on we were in our new parish. Just beyond Cache Creek a highway sign reads, "You Are Now Entering Historic Cariboo"—and historic it truly is.

The Cariboo is a vast, indefinite segment of British Columbia between Cache Creek and Prince George. Its life centers largely in the communities of Clinton, 100 Mile House, Williams Lake, and Quesnel, strung out in a line 265 miles long ending at the thriving city of Prince George. The eastern and western boundaries of the Cariboo are loosely defined simply because there is little in the outlying bush to establish any definite lines.

The first white man to see this country was Alexander Mackenzie, who led a party of nine men out of the Peace River district of Alberta to find a route to the Pacific Ocean. The men fought their way up what is now known as the Parsnip River and over the Canadian Rocky Mountains, descending the western slope by means of a series of connected lakes and streams until they came upon the Fraser River near the site of the present city of Prince George.

Setting out into the current of this great, unknown river, they guided their birch-bark canoe some eighty miles south. There Indians warned them that the river below was impassable. However, Mackenzie continued to a point on the river now marked on the map as Alexandria. There he became convinced that the Indians were correct and, with a native guide, turned north again to where the Blackwater River joins the Fraser. They paddled west toward the sea, but soon found the Blackwater unnavigable. Abandoning the canoe, Mackenzie trekked overland until he and his party of ragged, barefoot, and half-starved men finally reached the Pacific Ocean near the present site of Bella Coola. The date was July 19, 1793.

The rest of the Fraser River remained unexplored until

Simon Fraser, for whom the river was eventually named, set out from Fort Saint James in the autumn of 1807. He traveled the Nechako River to where it empties into the Fraser, and built Fort George, which is near Prince George. The explorer and his party spent the winter in the fort and in May of the next year moved out onto the great river in canoes. By June 1 they had reached the place where Mackenzie had turned back. But Fraser continued on, experiencing a succession of dangerous descents through the river's narrow gorges, with the men in almost constant peril. The struggle to keep afloat was frequently interrupted with exhausting portages around the most fearsome parts of the river. But they finally made their way past the mouth of the Thompson River, down Black Canyon, and past Hell's Gate. Suddenly, near the site of the present village of Yale, the river calmed down and broadened out and, thirty-five days after leaving Fort George, Fraser reached the sea at Vancouver.

Gold was discovered in the sand bars of the Thompson River in 1856. Men in search of the precious metal came by the thousands. They swarmed over the country of the Fraser and Thompson rivers and worked their way up tributary streams into the bushland of the Cariboo. Some struck it fabulously rich. Others nearly starved to death. Many lost their lives in the wild currents of the rivers or at the hands of hostile Indians. Most of them left the Cariboo with less than what they brought in, but the gold rush made one of the most colorful chapters in the history of British Columbia.

The lure of gold led men on into the mountains east of Quesnel, where Billy Barker found extensive deposits in a shaft dug into the bank of Williams Creek. By the following spring, six thousand miners were at work in the area, and for a while Barkerville was the largest town in British

Columbia. Today it is a ghost town, with just a few souls left to dream of the days when men made fortunes by day in the diggings and lost them by night in the saloons.

While Barkerville no longer thrives on gold, the Cariboo Gold Quartz Mining Company at Wells, five miles away, still produces the precious metal in sizable quantities. One day, when I was talking with the postmaster at Wells, he invited me to step into the back room of his little office. There on a table lay a small parcel wrapped in a bit of burlap. He invited me to pick it up and, when I was able to raise it off the table only with great effort, he told me that I held in my hands seventy-six pounds of pure gold, worth more than $30,000. I had thought that gold would be moved out of the Cariboo by armored car under heavy guard. But this shipment was going in the regular mail as an ordinary registered parcel. It was evidence that the frontier days were vanishing.

There are men who have never lost faith in the sands of the Cariboo country. Many of them sit out the bitter winters in little cabins here and there in the bush, perhaps doing a bit of trapping to eke out a living, and, when spring melts away the deep snows, set out with a fresh grubstake in the never-ending search for gold. They will tell you that somewhere in those hills there is still more to be found than the miners of a century ago ever took out.

All of this background we learned later from our reading.

From Cache Creek north our car sped along on a smooth new highway across the rolling hills of the southern Cariboo. The stretch of barren land was not extensive and soon we were driving through typical "bush" country—forests of spruce, fir, poplar, and birch, with frequent open meadows and small lakes. The poplar and birch trees were stripped of their leaves, for it was the last day of November and already the chill wind of winter had taken its toll. We noticed that the days were short, with not much more than seven hours of daylight, and that by four o'clock the sun had set and it was night.

At dark we reached 150 Mile House, a name that carries over from the days when the stagecoach drivers measured distance up the old Cariboo Road from Ashcroft on the Thompson River. We examined the map and found we were 160 miles from Prince George, our destination, and we decided that we could easily make it that evening.

Although it was dark, it was actually still early in the day and we expected to reach Prince George by seven thirty or eight o'clock. We had no sooner started on than, with a sudden jolt, the car made an unwelcome transition from smooth pavement to gravel. From then on, a narrow, winding road slowed our speed considerably. Frequent chuckholes lurked to jar the unwary traveler; so we advanced through the darkness with caution.

Mile after mile we went on, seeing nothing of the historic Cariboo except what the headlights revealed of the road ahead and the dense bush lining the way north. Occasionally, there were small clearings in the forest where dim lights flickered from the cabins of lumberjacks, trappers, and homesteaders who had come to stake their future on the development of still virgin land.

Darkness had been upon us for several hours when we entered the town of Quesnel. Its gay electric lights and paved streets gave brief evidence that civilization had at least gained a foothold in the Cariboo and that we had not left the modern world altogether behind. We should have spent the night there. But we drove on, impelled by some inner urge to reach our destination that evening. On through the darkness we went, over the hills, in and out of the canyons, sometimes near the ominous roar of the Fraser, and sometimes deep in the quiet forest.

The children had long been fast asleep on the back seat of the car. Virginia and I rode on in silent thought. Glancing at my wife, I noticed a tear trickle unchecked down her face. In a moment of fear I wondered what it meant. Was she disappointed in this country to which my rash telephone conversation had committed us? Did she already feel the lonesomeness that must come at some time to all women who face the wilderness?

"Virginia," I ventured, "are you sorry about our coming here?"

In silence I waited for the answer to my question. Then slowly she spoke, endeavoring to convey to me the depths of emotion that the beauty of the great forest had aroused.

"So many trees—the mountains—the lakes—and the streams! My heart is filled with peace. I'm sure I shall be happy here."

I felt the same.

Already, silently and almost imperceptibly, the fascination of the north had fixed itself upon us.

It was nearly midnight when we reached the edge of the hill overlooking Prince George. Its lights sparkled below us in a cheerful welcome. Winding down the hill, we quickly reached the Fraser River where, at the other end of a long bridge shared by the Canadian National Railway, we came to the "City Limits" sign. The streets were quite deserted at that hour, but we aroused a slumbering innkeeper, who soon made us comfortable for the remainder of the night, and wearily we fell asleep.

# 2

## PRINCE GEORGE

THE next morning we awoke to find that during the night the northland had been blanketed with white and that the green forests and meadows had been transformed into a fairyland of snowflakes and ice crystals.

Despite the change in the weather, we were warmly welcomed at Prince George. Brother and Sister George Toombs were the first to greet us and soon introduced us to the rest of the church members there. We found an active group of believers numbering about seventy-five, an attractive church building situated on a prominent street overlooking the city, and a thriving church school.

Within a week we had obtained a comfortable duplex apartment just one block from the church and school and were snugly settled for the long, cold winter months ahead. With housing cared for, I set out to explore my parish. First of all, I drove back south along the Cariboo Highway 190 miles to Lac la Hache, where a group of thirty-five Adventist sawmillers and their families had formed a church and were operating a little church school in the lumber camp. Sabbath services were held in the cookhouse dining room.

I decided to visit the Lamming Mills church on my next trip. The route from Prince George follows the Fraser River upstream. It starts northward but soon swings to east and then southeast in the direction of Jasper National Park. Since there was no road along the river, I had to go by train, a trip that took five hours whenever no serious trouble was encountered. Because of the mountainous terrain, the railway follows the river quite closely and the river is, in places, constantly undermining the track. The Canadian National Railway is forced to keep up an unceasing program of dumping trainload after trainload of rock into the roadbed to keep the river from destroying their track altogether.

The resulting unevenness of the track is the cause of rather frequent derailments and delays. On my first trip to Lamming Mills, the passenger train on which I was riding pulled up behind a freight train that had been derailed. When it became obvious that we were faced with a long delay, I asked the conductor how far we were from Lamming Mills. When he told me that it was only two miles, I picked up my small suitcase and started walking along the track. Forty minutes later I trudged around a curve and came in sight of the little shed that serves as the railway station for the lumber camp, which is located on a flat overlooking the river.

I had previously sent word that I was coming, and, since it was my first visit, there was a welcoming committee awaiting me at the station. Some surprised looks appeared on the faces of the group as they realized that their new pastor was not arriving by train. Some, at first, even believed that

I had actually walked the 170 miles from Prince George!

The Lamming Mills church, with a membership that has now grown to almost two hundred baptized believers, is the largest in the district. In spite of its lonely isolation, this group is keenly interested in the world field and carries on an active program of assisting the denomination in all of its mission endeavors.

In addition to the three organized churches in the district, we found a small company of believers meeting for Sabbath school in the home of Brother Conn Reyse at Quesnel. There were other Adventists in the north, but information as to their whereabouts was often vague. We found them one by one, or a family or two at a time, all the way from Cache Creek to Fort Saint John.

Dan Basaraba and the Jacobson brothers, Harold and Odt, moved into the Cariboo with their logging and sawmill crews about the same time we arrived and we were soon visiting them as regularly as we could. Brother Basaraba set up his mill sixteen miles south of Williams Lake on the Dog Creek road, and the Jacobsons located at the head of Beaver Valley seven miles from the little community of Horsefly.

Before the winter was over we had found, to our happy surprise, nearly five hundred Sabbathkeepers in our wilderness parish.

The beginning of the history of Seventh-day Adventists in the northern interior of British Columbia centered mainly in the Prince George area. In 1921 Brother George Brown, who was interested in purchasing property in the north, made a trip through to Prince George. He carried with him a prospectus and took orders for our books in the homes of many of the people that he visited. After returning from the north, he arranged for Brother George Toombs, who was then serving as the publishing secretary for the British Columbia Conference, to go and make the deliveries.

In the course of his canvassing work, Brother Brown met two families in Prince George, the Prossers and the Lottmans, who were both Seventh-day Adventists, each family thinking that they were the only believers in the town. He introduced the two families to each other, and later, when Brother Toombs came to deliver the books Brother Brown had sold, they were organized into the first Sabbath school in Prince George. They met in the home of the Lottmans.

As Brother Toombs traveled through the north in 1921 he was greatly impressed with the needs and possibilities for our work there, and, when he returned to his home and told his wife what he had seen, they covenanted together that, when the opportunity came, they would settle in the north to engage in self-supporting missionary work.

The years came and went until 1942 found Brother and Sister Toombs living in Armstrong, British Columbia, where Brother Toombs and his son Irving were engaged in the painting trade. One day a representative of the Fuller Brush Company approached Brother Toombs and talked to him about becoming a salesman for their company. The Toombses were not much interested until this gentleman volunteered the information that, if they would accept the proposition, he would give them the Cariboo for their territory.

They asked for a little time to think it over. However, in the meantime, another man took the opening and went north. But he soon quit, and again the Fuller Brush Company came to George Toombs, offering him not only the Cariboo district, but also the territory west and east of Prince George. This time they were ready to accept.

With a second-hand car and a house trailer purchased from the proceeds of the sale of their home, Brother and

Sister Toombs drove into the Cariboo with the professed intention of selling Fuller brushes, but actually to fulfill their dream of giving the advent message to the isolated people of the interior. They carried literature, placing some in most of the homes they visited. Selling brushes to earn a living, they sought for and found opportunities to hold Bible studies.

That first summer they worked their way west from Prince George to Burns Lake, then south across François Lake and down deep into the bush along the shores of Ootsa Lake. There they met John Anderson, a bachelor, and found that he had been keeping the seventh-day Sabbath for seven years. Overjoyed with this discovery, Brother Toombs inquired as to how John Anderson had learned the Sabbath truth. He was told of a neighbor, Olaf Bjerken, living not far away, who had observed the Sabbath for fourteen years!

Brother and Sister Toombs met Olaf Bjerken and heard him relate his experience of receiving, from an Adventist brother passing through the bush country, a single copy of *The Review and Herald*. This particular copy of *The Review* contained the account of a miraculous healing from cancer. This story so impressed him that Olaf Bjerken decided that the people who published that paper had something for him. He studied that one paper and accepted all the light that it contained.

Now these two brethren accepted the full Adventist message and requested baptism. As their life in the bush was a hard struggle financially, neither of the men had sufficient money to travel any distance to meet one of our pastors. Perhaps their isolation can best be described by the difficulties they experienced in uniting with the church. When the conference knew of their desire to be baptized, a minister was sent north by train and a letter was dispatched asking

Mr. Anderson and Mr. Bjerken to meet him at Burns Lake on the rail line. But by the time they had received the letter at Ootsa Lake the minister had come and gone. This happened several times before they finally succeeded in receiving baptism.

In the fall the Toombses returned to Prince George, bought a little piece of land on the outskirts of the city, and built a rough shelter over their house trailer for the winter. Later they moved the trailer out and added on to the shelter. The place where the trailer stood that first winter is the living room of their present home.

I once asked Sister Toombs how she had felt about leaving a comfortable home and going north to the rugged life she has lived there since. She told me that she had made the move to Prince George the subject of earnest prayer, and once in the north was so impressed by its needs that, like it or not, she had determined to stay.

Prior to 1942, Elder Ainsley Blair had held a series of evangelistic meetings in Prince George and several had accepted the message. However, Elder Blair could not stay with the converts, and, by the time the Toombses arrived in the summer of 1942, the little group had become almost inactive. The first Sabbath they were in the north, Brother and Sister Toombs conducted Sabbath school in the morning at the home of a family by the name of Sherman, and again in the afternoon at the home of Brother and Sister Erickson.

Soon the believers, encouraged by again having some leadership, decided to meet together and, for want of a better place, conducted their first services in the open air not far from the site of the present church building.

After World War II the Prince George group purchased an army canteen building, moved it to town, and converted it into a comfortable and commodious place of worship.

As we visited from place to place we, too, sensed the possibilities of evangelism in the north. We knew that there would be no large audiences or blazing headlines, but felt that many would respond if we brought the message to them. Somehow, at camp meeting that summer, the other conference workers dubbed me the "king of the north." However, contrary to the Biblical prediction that "he shall come to his end, and none shall help him," the conference committee sent Brother and Sister John Holstein back with us to assist in the work. They willingly and successfully adjusted themselves to the conditions in the north and proved a great blessing to us. We held four evangelistic campaigns together that winter and God gave us forty-one souls for our hire.

The long distances between places, the rough roads, and the extreme cold in the winter made the work hard, but we encouraged one another and kept going. There were times when we really couldn't have gotten along without each other. That winter was a bitter one, with the temperature ranging from 20° to 40° below zero for weeks at a time. Day after day we had trouble getting our cars started, but it never failed that when mine wouldn't start, John's would, and when his wouldn't start, mine would. Then whichever car started would be used to push the other, until we had both vehicles running and thus could carry on with our appointments for Bible studies and meetings for the day.

Sometimes out on the bush roads a car wouldn't have sufficient traction in the snow without additional weight over the rear wheels. John and I would take turns riding on the rear bumper, changing off to drive the car when fingers and ears and nose were close to freezing. When John and I had to be away from home for extended periods of time, Cynthia, his wife, and Virginia found comfort in one another's companionship.

During that winter we held some meetings in the public schoolhouse at Little Prairie, two hundred miles north of Prince George on the other side of the Continental Divide, where the rivers flow east and north, finally reaching Beaufort Sea and the Arctic Ocean. John and I were driving along the road not far from the schoolhouse one morning when we noticed the lone figure of a man walking toward us. As we drew nearer, we could see that it was a young man dressed in thin, tattered clothes, and walking with a slight limp. He was pulling a sled behind him loaded with a pitiful-looking little mound of personal belongings. It was 20° below zero.

When we came close enough to see the features of his face, John instantly recognized the young man. It was Ted (not his true name), who had once been a schoolmate of his at Canadian Union College. We stopped and John got out of the car to talk to him. At first Ted tried to hide his identity and denied that he had ever known John. But John, in his kindly way, insisted and soon had the shivering man seated in our warm car.

As soon as John had introduced Ted to me I realized that I already knew much of the young man's background. Brought up in an Adventist home in Prince George, Ted had attended our college for a while, then had become discouraged and quit school. Perhaps the loss of his father in a tragic logging accident had contributed to his attitude toward life in general.

Ted turned his back on the church and, as he mingled with questionable associates of the world, it was not long until he was in trouble with the law. He served a term in the penitentiary. Then, feeling that he had disgraced his widowed mother, he disappeared. One of the most faithful attendants at prayer meeting in Prince George was Ted's mother. Week after week this loving, loyal mother requested us to join her in prayer that somehow God would lead her son back home again. She did not know where he was.

There in the car beside the road Ted haltingly began to tell us what had happened since he had left home. He had gone to another province, where he had obtained work in the oil fields. One day, while he was working on a drilling operation, his foot was painfully injured. After restless weeks in a hospital, he left before the wound had fully healed. Hence the limp.

He had reached Little Prairie penniless, cold, and hungry, without home or friend, and had finally been offered shelter by some kindly Indians. When we found him on the road he was on his way to their log cabin in the bush. All of his earthly possessions were on the little sled he was dragging along behind him.

I told him of how his mother had prayed for him through the years. Gently John and I pleaded with him to go home. We told him that we were leaving for Prince George that very night after the evening service and that he could ride with us. For a long while we all sat in silence as a great struggle raged in Ted's mind. Then, with tears in his eyes, he voiced his decision. He would go with us.

That night we were on our way by nine-thirty, and with a two-hundred-mile journey before us we had plenty of time to talk. We discussed many things, but mostly Ted brought the conversation back to his own needs and problems. He had learned the hard way that it didn't pay to turn one's back upon God and a Christian mother.

Shortly after two o'clock in the morning we entered the silent streets of Prince George and soon turned into a driveway familiar to the young man. As Ted looked at the house that had been home to him before the wasted years, he shrank back in fear. Instead of getting out of the car, he remained seated with his head buried in his hands and told us that he couldn't face his mother.

I got out of the car, knocked sharply on the door of the house until Ted's mother was aroused, and then asked her to remain at the door for a moment until I returned. Back at the car, I took the young man by the hand and led him to the house. In a flash the mother had her son clasped in her arms. She brushed aside his stammering confession of the wrong he had done her, and there in the night the tears of joy flowed freely. John and I felt the scene too sacred for any further intrusion, and we slipped unnoticed out of the yard, only glad to know that a lonely mother's prayers for her wayward son had at last been answered.

It had not taken long for the north to prove that our call to this district had truly been a call to adventure—adventure for the church and for God. Day by day we felt the warmth of soul that comes from having a part in the lives of those who so much appreciated the spiritual help a pastor could bring to them.

True to his word, Elder Smithwick soon offered us the pastorate of a city church. We thanked him for remembering his promise, but assured him that now our hearts were in the north—we could not leave our wilderness parish.

# 3

## BUMP—400 FEET

I ONCE gave the northland a glowing build-up in a report to a friend of mine who lived in a large city, and suggested that he load his family into the car and come up for his holidays. He had been smart enough to ask me about the roads and I had assured him that they weren't bad—mostly dirt and gravel, but not really bad at all. The roads of the Cariboo country are most difficult to describe. The fact that I'd been in trouble over this before should have taught me to leave the subject alone.

His car, a small European model of rather ancient vintage, just couldn't take the shaking up it received. It barely limped home from the trip, with some burned valves and quite a collection of squeaks and rattles. For a while I was afraid that my friend was not going to speak to me again, but fortunately he was of a forgiving spirit.

Any person who has lived in the Cariboo understands all

too well about the roads. But I soon learned that, when
giving information to strangers, all remarks had to be quali-
fied. I eventually came to think of a road as being in fair
condition if it was passable without pushing or pulling, and
naturally it was only fair to explain this to the uninitiated.

One time, when John Holstein and I were planning to
hold some evangelistic meetings in the town of McBride
near Lamming Mills, we decided that we should take a car
in with us. Ordinarily we rode the train from Prince George
directly to the mill, a route that followed up the Fraser River
where for about one hundred miles there is no automobile
road at all. Since the cost of taking a car on the train was
prohibitive, we had to find a way to drive in. We learned
that a bush road following the Thompson River north from
a settlement called Blue River had just recently been opened
to traffic and that, by following a very circuitous route for
525 miles, it was possible to drive into Lamming Mills.

Just north of the settlement of Little Fort, on our trip
up the Blue River Road, we noticed a car parked beside the
road. The occupants of the car had spread their lunch out
on the grass at the edge of a little mountain brook and were
eating their midday meal. As we went by, I recognized
familiar faces and stopped our car.

Pastor Russell Spangler and his family had been in to
the mill to visit relatives and were now on their way out.
I asked him how he liked the Blue River country. But he
brushed my question aside and with a feeling of deep conviction told me, "This is the worst road I have ever been on!"

As proof, he proffered for my inspection a collection of
automotive parts that had worked loose along the way and
which he had completely removed for safekeeping. I quickly
assured him that the north had roads still worse, and encouraged him not to feel too glum about his troubles.

Actually the Blue River Road isn't bad. If one doesn't exceed twenty miles per hour there are few spots that could be considered really rough. The soil is, for the most part, sandy, and therefore few deep mudholes develop even during very heavy rains. However, the road is very narrow in many places and there seem to be an endless number of turns. Fortunately, traffic is light and the chance of a head-on collision on a blind curve is not great. In winter the road is closed by snow.

The scenery along the Blue River Road is magnificent. Following the course of the North Thompson River until the stream disappears into a group of glacier-clad mountains, the road leads through a wild, rugged country. For miles the traveler is hidden under the dense foliage of giant cedar trees, which forever shut out any direct sunlight from the floor of the forest. I have driven through this forest in the night and found the darkness so intense that I had the eerie feeling of being absolutely alone and shut away from the rest of the world. Huge ferns decorate the landscape, and thick green moss carpets the ground.

The men who build and maintain the roads of the Cariboo are a resourceful, hard-working lot. They do a magnificent job considering the tremendous odds against which they work. Serving a sparsely populated area spread out over thousands of square miles of some of the most difficult road-building terrain in the world, they tackle their job with a minimum of money and equipment. Heroic is actually the word for the crew members, who stay on the job summer or winter, regardless of the weather, to keep a way open for travelers through the wilderness of mountains and forests, across countless streams and rivers, and over or around the spongy swamps.

One brief stroke of nature often undoes in a few moments

the accomplishments of months of sweat and toil. A thirty-minute cloudburst once washed out nearly every bridge between Prince George and Quesnel and marooned us from the rest of the world for ten days until the road crews were able to build temporary crossings out of huge logs placed across the deep, washed-out gullies left by the storm.

The Department of Highways of the Province of British Columbia is now building a new, wide, and well-graded highway all the way to Prince George. When it is completed it will be as modern and smooth as any highway and will undoubtedly do much to open up this country to thousands of new settlers. To the south of the Cariboo, the Fraser Canyon highway is also being rebuilt, and the result will be a safe as well as scenic passage through that wild gorge. But I'm glad I saw the north before all of this happened. It will never be quite the same again.

On the back roads the traveler is usually left to the fate of his own judgment regarding the hazards that lie ahead. But the main thoroughfare, the Cariboo Highway, is well marked and, if the driver will obey the signs, little serious trouble should be experienced. One of the road signs most frequently seen is the bump warning. If the bump is just reasonably rough, the sign reads quite sedately "BUMP—400 FEET." But if the spot ahead is really grim, the sign is significantly printed "**BUMP** —400 FEET." It means slow down—or else!

Most of the bumps are the result of spring breakup. During the winter the ground freezes four to ten feet deep, depending upon the severity of the weather and the amount of moisture present in the soil. When spring with its milder temperatures arrives, the frost begins to work out of the ground. This thawing action makes the roadbed a soft, oozing mass of mud which soon causes the surface layer of gravel or hard surfacing to break up, wreaking havoc with the highway.

One year the spring thaw was so devastating that the road crews had to pave the Cariboo Highway with heavy planks for several miles in order to keep traffic moving. To save the roads as much as possible from such damage, the use of all trucks is banned for about a month every spring.

Experience taught us to be prepared for almost any kind of road emergency. Together with Virginia and the girls, I had been making calls in the Williams Lake district one day. About nine o'clock in the evening we decided to drive the sixteen miles out from town to spend the night at Dan Basaraba's lumber camp. It was during spring breakup, but we didn't anticipate much difficulty getting out there as it was still early in the season.

A little over two miles from camp the road crosses an open field. When we got to that point, we found it impassable. Somehow we backed out of the mud we had driven into and, once again on more sold ground, looked around to see if there was some other way that we could go. We finally noticed some car tracks leading off at the edge of the field and hope-fully followed them through the darkness. We had gone barely a hundred yards when the headlights of the car revealed a quagmire of mud ahead so forbidding that we unanimously decided to go back to town and spend the night in a motel.

I successfully turned the car around, but had not pro-ceeded far when the right rear wheel, sinking deep in the ooze, got wedged in between some tree roots. We were stopped in our tracks, and no amount of spinning the wheels or pushing would budge us. We worked until we had tried everything we could think of to free the car from the en-tanglement, but without success.

We discussed walking the remaining two miles to camp. But we were already so spattered with mud that we couldn't bear to think of stumbling up that road in the pitch dark. Besides, it was midnight and we were exhausted. So we crawled into the car and tried to sleep, waiting until daylight would give us a chance to see what we were doing.

Fortunately the temperature dropped below the freezing point during the remainder of the night and by morning the mud was stiff enough from the cold to enable us to be out and on our way with a minimum of effort. We drove home to Prince George that morning and spent the rest of the day getting cleaned up.

Wheel bearings gave us considerable trouble. No doubt the succession of snow, mud, rain, and dust is hard on every moving part of an automobile. These conditions, added to the constant pounding of rough roads, resulted in the necessity for frequent repairs. Often many parts of the car moved that were never intended to move and the punishment our machines underwent was terrific. For every day we were in the Cariboo I drove an average of one hundred miles, and I wore out a new car every year.

My first experience with wheel bearings came on the way home from Dawson Creek one cold winter day. John Holstein was with me. We had reached a lonely section of road in the foothills of the Rocky Mountains when we suddenly heard an ominous clatter in the rear of the car. I stopped to investigate the cause of the noise and found that the left rear wheel was warm. We suspected bearing trouble, but were not absolutely sure that that was our problem.

As there was really nothing that we could do about it there, we decided to drive on slowly and see if we could make it to Little Prairie, where a mechanic operated a small garage. At first everything was fairly quiet, but a few miles farther on our hopefulness was shattered by another burst of noise. We stopped again and found the wheel almost too hot to touch. It was quite evident that the bearing was being ground to bits and that each turn of the wheel was only making the situation worse. But by alternately proceeding very slowly and then stopping awhile to let the wheel cool, we did make it to Little Prairie.

The mechanic at the garage pulled the wheel off for us but, of course, did not have the parts necessary to repair the damage. He gave us a list of the required items and we set off for Prince George, the most likely place to obtain them. There were three ways of getting there now that we didn't have our own transportation. We could walk. But neither of us fancied a two-hundred-mile hike across the mountains in the dead of winter. There was a bus that came through three times a week, but it just happened that we would have to wait nearly two days for the next trip through. The only remaining way was to hitchhike.

Traffic in that part of the country is light at any time of the year, but now that it was winter there were very few cars making the trip through to Prince George. However, we rather optimistically walked out to the road and began waiting. We waited and waited! A chilly wind was blowing off the icy slopes of the Rockies to add to our discomforting situation, and we tried to keep warm by pacing up and down the road. A few local vehicles on short errands went by, but it seemed as though nobody was going to Prince George that day.

After a couple of hours we were so cold that we walked over to a little café to find something to eat and to get warmed up. While we were there a gentleman and his wife stopped for a meal. Overhearing their conversation, we could tell that they were driving through to the south and, when we explained our plight to them, they very kindly offered us a ride. For this courtesy we were extremely thankful, and we arrived at Prince George that evening.

There was a bus going north early the next morning but now I had the problem of obtaining the needed parts for the car after the shops were closed for the day. Providentially, we had been in Prince George only a few moments when I met the salesman who had sold me my car. He went immediately to the garage for which he worked and found the parts for me that evening. By the next night we were mobile again.

These early experiences in the north led to the accumulation of a large number of items which became standard equipment in our travels throughout the district. Needless to say, I always carried an extra wheel-bearing set after that first one burned out. Then I added spare ignition parts, a spare fan belt, an extra spare tire, with tire irons, air pump, and tube patching kit, a new muffler, and extra exhaust gaskets. In addition, I carried extra oil for the engine, a can of hydraulic brake fluid, and a five-gallon can of gasoline.

For getting out of mudholes or snowbanks I kept in the trunk of the car a shovel, a length of stout tow rope, and tire chains. Trees sometimes fell across the bush roads during storms; so I added an ax and a saw to the equipment. I also learned to carry a suit of work clothes to which I could change when the situation demanded it. To these items I added a sleeping bag, a small box of nonperishable foods for emergency rations, and a good flashlight. Sooner or later each piece of equipment played its useful part in keeping the work going in the northland.

One of the most useful things I carried was a block of wood about a foot square and two inches thick. It made a firm foundation for the jack and often enabled me to raise our car out of the mud when the jack itself would have sunk into the mire. When no help was at hand to tow the car out of a mudhole, we followed the procedure of jacking each wheel up as high as possible and then spreading out thick evergreen branches underneath. This would form a matting that kept the wheels from sinking back too deeply into the mud when the jack was removed. Then, cutting more branches, which were usually available close by, we would place a layer of them on the mud ahead of the car. With this done, we could usually drive on to firmer ground. So the block of wood was very important!

It was not always the most desirable thing to be towed out of a mudhole. One day when I had failed to negotiate an unusually bad stretch of private logging road, a truck came up behind me. The driver kindly offered to help me out. As he couldn't get by my car to tow it through forward, we fastened the cable onto the rear of the car and pulled it out backward. As we did so, the end of the exhaust pipe on my car became entangled with some tree roots and both the pipe and the muffler were pulled loose from the engine and were wrapped around the rear axle. You can imagine what it looked like after that! At any rate, we got the car out to where the truck could get by, and then the driver hooked on again and pulled me back through the mud in the direction I wanted to go. I repaired the muffler later on.

In summer, when the roads were dry, the most annoying problems were the clouds of dust and the flying pieces of gravel kicked up by passing vehicles. Time after time the windshield of my car was shattered by rocks. I came to follow the practice of not having the glass replaced until it was really dangerous to drive with it.

Speaking of gravel, an unusual experience happened to

John and me as we were traveling from Williams Lake to Prince George late one night in his car. We had descended the treacherous hill into Cottonwood Canyon and were climbing out on the other side when the engine began to knock noisily. We immediately checked the oil-pressure gauge and found that it registered zero. After a look at the dip stick on the motor revealed not a trace of lubricant, John crawled under the car to investigate and discovered the crankcase drain plug hanging by the last thread. Fortunately it was still there, but it had loosened enough to allow all of the oil to leak out. Evidently some careless mechanic had failed to tighten the plug securely after changing the oil, and the constant banging and scraping of the bottom of the car on the deep, loose gravel over which we had driven had worked the plug loose. As John had not taken the precaution of carrying extra oil, we turned the car around by pushing it and coasted back down into the canyon, where there was a little store and gas station. It was after midnight, but we succeeded in arousing the storekeeper, who obligingly supplied our needs. John tightened the drain plug securely and added the oil. Then, with some anxiety, he started the engine which, to our great relief, purred as smoothly as ever. We were glad that it had all turned out so happily.

Under these conditions of travel we endeavored to carry on the work that had been placed in our care. We always felt that God was with us through every difficulty and, in spite of the fact that much of our time was spent in just getting from one place to another, we were blessed with encouraging results for the effort.

Many of the new members added to the church by baptism were what we called "isolated believers," which simply means that they lived where it was impossible for them to attend a regular church service. But we tried to bring the message to those who showed an interest, no matter how widely scattered they might be.

For example, in the spring of 1958 I was studying with sixteen people who were preparing for baptism. One day each week I drove 203 miles in order to meet with a young lady who lived near Quesnel. Another day took me on a 128-mile round trip into the bush near Horsefly to study with a family who owned a cattle ranch there. Still another study was conducted weekly at Lac la Hache, which involved a trip of 120 miles and, in addition, there was a family out to the west of Williams Lake which meant another 150 miles. But the results far outweighed the cost in time and effort. Down at the conference office the brethren did their best to stretch the budget to help meet the expense, and God gave the increase.

Sometimes we were asked why we ventured out even when we knew that the roads were next to impassable. We went simply because there never was a time when conditions were ideal, and nothing could be accomplished by sitting at home when there was so much to be done and so little time in which to do it.

# 4

## THE TIME THE ANGELS PUSHED

THE road north from Prince George crosses the Nechako River at the edge of the city and immediately leads off into a wild, sparsely settled bush country. Indians, trappers, and a few hardy souls who cater to the needs of travelers make up the bulk of the population. The great Hudson's Bay Company, which has taken largely to the cities for its business enterprises now, still maintains a number of trading posts in Indian territory, and one of these can be visited near McLeod Lake about ninety miles out from Prince George.

For the first one hundred miles north the route follows quite closely the series of lakes and streams which bore the explorer Alexander Mackenzie and his party out of Alberta's Peace River country in the year 1793 in their search for a waterway to the Pacific Ocean. The waters of the north connect areas so vast as to be fantastic in size. Backtracking down the Parsnip River along Mackenzie's route, one could enter the Peace River, and from there go into Great Slave Lake. Following the shores of this immense lake to its outlet, the traveler could float down the Mackenzie River all the way to the Arctic Ocean.

But crossing the Parsnip River on a modern bridge a few miles beyond the Hudson's Bay Company's trading post at McLeod Lake, the road veers to the east and climbs into the pass that leads through the Rocky Mountains. Although Pine Pass, as it is called, is not a high one, the mountain scenery presents views of the rugged rock masses so typical of the Rockies.

Once over the mountains, the road descends into an entirely different type of country. Below the foothills, the thick bush thins out and the land levels off into the open prairies of the Peace River district. In spite of the long, bitterly cold winters, these northern prairies are settled by farmers with a pioneering spirit, who sow the vast stretches of land with grain and, if the weather holds right, reap bountiful harvests from the fertile soil.

Dawson Creek, for many years a small frontier community, has recently mushroomed into a thriving city. Aided by the building of the Alaska Highway and the discovery of oil in the north, it has become the most important center of business in British Columbia north of Prince George.

We made our first trip into the Peace River section of our parish during the month of February, 1955. On this trip we were able to visit several isolated families of church members, who seemed to appreciate a call from an Adventist minister. One of our first calls was near the village of Little Prairie, which is situated in the eastern foothills of the Rocky Mountains. We had heard that two families, the Nichols and the Mortons, were operating a small sawmill at Big Lake about twenty-five miles from Little Prairie. To find their place, we were directed several miles north along the highway and then off on a side road into the bush.

Although it was not late in the day, the winter sun had dropped below the horizon. Snow lay deep over the countryside and, with the mercury standing at 20° below zero, the northland was in the grip of winter. Coming to the place to which we had been directed, we turned off onto the bush road. A quarter of a mile later a bend in that road seemed as though it shut us off completely from the highway we had just left and a dark, cold wilderness closed in behind us.

Mile after mile we drove on through the darkness. The road was narrow and winding and unfamiliar. Progress was slow. Apparently a bulldozer, pushing through the bush, had knocked the trees to one side and then hurried on without stopping to do much else to make the road passable. It was evident that very little traffic moved in and out of the area and, at places, drifted snow almost stopped us completely. But we kept going. Coming to a fork in the road, we searched for some indication as to which way to turn, but there was not so much as a blazed tree to mark the direction to the camp. After some hesitation, we blindly decided to take the left road and hoped that we would find a house where we could ask for further directions.

About two hours after leaving the highway we came to another fork in the road. We were now twenty miles deep in the bush and had not seen a trace of human habitation in all of those dark miles. If we were on the right road, we knew that we must be close to the Nichol-Morton camp, but again there was no indication as to which way we should turn. Fearing to get stuck in the darkness and the sub-zero weather on a dead-end trail with no room to turn around, we decided to leave the car at the fork and walk a short distance to see what we could find. Each of us would take a different direction and the first one to spot a house would return to the car and give a long blast on the horn.

Taking the left-hand fork, I had walked less than half a mile when I saw, in the distance, a faint, flickering light. I hurried back to the car and sounded the signal. We were soon on our way toward the camp. Our arrival was quite a surprise, but we were given a hearty welcome and ushered into the Nichols' home, where the family was gathered around a red-hot wood heater endeavoring to keep themselves warm. We also met the Morton family that evening, and had a very enjoyable visit with them.

These folk had recently left the prairies of Saskatchewan and moved west to establish themselves in the sawmill business. Having little capital for such a venture, they had courageously moved into this isolated place where timber was cheap. Living in rough cabins, they were struggling against the difficulties of primitive pioneer life. However, we found them enjoying a good Christian experience and, although so very much alone, maintaining a keen interest in the work of the church. They faithfully gathered each week for Sabbath school.

We again had the privilege of visiting these families and becoming better acquainted with them during the next winter. Several of the children were old enough to think seriously of preparing for baptism. When the subject was brought up, they responded readily. We talked it over and decided that I should plan to return during the next summer, when a baptism could be conducted in the lake beside their camp.

It seemed best to make this trip before we had to leave for camp meeting in the south. However, because spring breakup comes even later in the Peace River country than in the Cariboo, I waited as long as possible on account of the bad roads. Toward the end of June I headed north from Prince George back over the Rocky Mountains to Little Prairie. The main highway leading through Pine Pass was in fair condition and I hoped that the bush road into the Big Lake camp would be dried up and passable by the time that I got there.

I drove through Little Prairie and soon turned off the highway onto the camp road. I was surprised to find myself traveling over a newly graded and well-drained road and happily anticipated an easy trip to the sawmill. A half mile from the highway I met a man operating a grader and stopped to ask him what was happening. He told me that he was improving the road for the use of a crew that was building a railway through that section of country. Eventually there would be a good road almost all of the twenty miles to the sawmill camp, but now he had just begun his work and, unfortunately, there was less than a mile of the job completed. He assured me that beyond that point the road was still very muddy from spring breakup and quite impassable.

However, feeling that my trip was a very important one, I refused to take his word about the road ahead and drove on until the improved section ended in a large mudhole. I stopped the car to survey the situation. After poking around in the mud with a stick to find out how far it was down to solid ground, I decided that it would be possible to get through. I tossed several armloads of evergreen branches into the mud and, backing off to get a good run at it, splashed and spun the car through the hole.

With intermittent patches of solid ground, I made it through a succession of smaller mudholes until I was confronted by a stretch of mire nearly a hundred yards long. I debated for some time over the possibility of getting through successfully, and almost wished that I had taken the road grader's advice and turned back while the going was good. Finally, I decided that I should give it a try.

Throttle to the floor, I drove into the hole and, using every bit of bush-road skill that I had acquired, got about halfway through before the car mired down and refused to move either forward or backward. Every effort to move the car only spun the wheels and dug them in deeper. The left side of the car was down so far into the mud that I couldn't open the door on that side, but I crawled out the right door to look the situation over. It appeared so hopeless that I decided to walk the remaining seventeen miles to camp, leaving the car where it was. Later on I could get some help to move it.

Anticipating just such a situation, I had brought along my pack board and now got it out of the trunk and began to fasten my sleeping bag, toilet articles, and books in place for the long hike ahead of me. I did not mind the walking, but it was late in the afternoon and I knew that it would be midnight before I could reach the camp. This was wild country, and wolves, bears, and other large animals prowled the forest in search of prey. Merlin, one of the Nichol boys, making this same trip on foot one night, had been followed closely by a cougar for several miles.

When I had completed my preparations and was ready to leave the car behind, the thought came to my mind that I should first ask the Lord to help me get the car out of that mud hole. Then, if He did not see fit to answer this prayer, I would understand that He wanted me to walk to the camp, which I was quite willing to do.

I got back into the driver's seat, placed the loaded pack board beside me, and then bowed my head, making a simple request that, if it were His will, God would move my car out onto solid ground.

Starting the engine, I shifted to low gear and let the clutch take hold. It seemed like such a foolish thing to do after all the times I had vainly tried the same thing just a few moments before. But, to my amazement, the wheels did not even so much as spin the least bit and, surely, steadily, the car moved forward and out of the mud!

There was no visible help, and I was certain that God had miraculously answered my prayer. With no other possible explanation of what had happened, I could only come to the conclusion that angels had been sent to push my car through. Now I knew that nothing could stop me, and confidently I drove on through mudhole after mudhole, never fearful of getting stuck again on that trip. Going around one bend, I surprised a great black bear sitting in the middle of the road, and was thankful to be in the car and not afoot in the lengthening shadows of evening!

At last the miles passed by and I arrived at my destination. At the camp I was told that no one had driven over that road for weeks and that it was still considered impassable even for trucks. Everyone was surprised that I had been able to get through.

The next morning we began Bible classes for the young folk, five of whom were planning for baptism. In the evenings everyone, young and old, gathered in one home for singing and study. It was a wonderful week—one of the most enjoyable of my ministry.

As the week drew to a close, we selected for the baptism a spot along the lake shore near the Morton home. After a service held in the house, we walked down to the water. I had instructed the folk to sing while the baptism proceeded, but, as the candidates one by one received the sacred rite,

I noticed that the singing was getting weaker and weaker until it faded out altogether.

Glancing up at the little audience witnessing the ceremony, I noticed that tears were flowing freely and that no one was really able to sing. So we completed the service without music, and then went back to the house. On the way up the path I noticed that the father of three of the young people just baptized was deeply moved. I wondered if, perhaps, something other than joy was causing the manifestation of his feelings.

But, looking my way, he sensed my question and assured me, "I'm so happy—so very happy!"

# 5

## BUSH CABIN

THE quiet of the bush was disturbed by the ring of hammers and shouts of "Bring that two-by-four!" "Please hold this board." "Where is the level?" And "Some more nails, please!"

By a small lake deep in the forest on the timber holdings of Dan Basaraba, and sixteen miles from the nearest town, we were busy building a home for ourselves. The sounds of saw and hammer came from no contractor's experienced crew—this was strictly a family affair. Virginia and the girls donned work clothes and wielded carpenter's tools with enthusiasm as, board by board, nail by nail, we put together a three-room cabin that we were to call home for two years.

In June of 1956 a meeting had been held in Williams Lake to which all of our church members in the area were invited. A large group gathered and, with Elder Smithwick and Elder W. A. Nelson, the Canadian Union Conference

*The suspension bridge over the Fraser
River near the town of Williams Lake.*

*The church school at Basaraba's lumber
camp which Kathy and Carolynn attended two years.*

Our portable home-built cabin at the
Basaraba camp.  Note the fancy front door.

Virginia Cooper smiles over a tempting
pail of blueberries gathered in the bush.

The massive ice formations which
are to be seen along the Fraser River canyon.

Our first boat, in which we explored
many of the lakes of the Cariboo.

*One of several cars which
were worn out running
100 miles per day in the bush.*

*Primitive cooking in the depth of the bush can still produce a very tempting meal.*

*Carolynn and Kathy on a trapper's trail in the dense cedar forest of Wells Gray Park.*

*The boat we launched in Summit Lake,*
*near Prince George at an old Indian village.*

*Three caribou—father, mother, and young—*
*swimming in Azure Lake, Wells Gray Park.*

*Virginia watches the girls*
*wading in Clearwater Lake;*
*Mount Buchanan in the background.*

*A part of the sawmill operated by
the Jacobson brothers in Beaver Valley.*

*Winter logging operations at Lamming Mills,*
*British Columbia, conducted by Adventists.*

*Virginia relaxes near a deserted*
*trapper's cabin found on the shore of Horsefly Lake.*

*Pastor Cooper shaves with ice-cold water and other*
*conveniences of the bushland.*

*The home in Prince George, enjoyed*
*after the years spent in the cabin at Basaraba's.*

*The desolate stretch of Coast
Mountains on the 300-mile
trip west to Bella Coola.*

*Repairing the washout that terminated progress on the trip to Bella Coola.*

president, presiding, formal action was taken to organize the Williams Lake Seventh-day Adventist church. It was a happy day for all of us, for now the believers could look forward to coming in from the lumber camps on Sabbath to unite in worship and to enjoy each other's fellowship. Some had to travel as far as fifty miles to get to the services, but Sabbath became a real high day in the lives of our people. Regardless of the weather or road conditions, there was always a good attendance.

At first the newly organized church met in a rented lodge hall, and one of the main projects to be considered was the erection of a building of their own. Eventually a fine piece of property was located and construction begun.

Since the church members planned to do most of the work themselves, I wanted to help as much as possible. At that time the 160 miles of road between Prince George and Williams Lake was gravel, and rough almost all the way; so Virginia and I talked it over and decided that it would be best if we left Prince George and located our home in the Williams Lake area.

The first problem to be solved was the education of our girls, for we did not wish to send them to public school. There was, as yet, no church school right in the town, but Brother Dan Basaraba and his crew had built a school at their lumber camp and had hired a teacher for their children. We approached Mr. Basaraba on the subject and he very generously gave us permission to live at his camp.

We would have to build our own cabin in the bush and learn a completely new way of living. But we were game and looked forward eagerly to the challenge of the experience. Besides making it possible for the girls to continue their training in the atmosphere of a Christian school, it would give us a real insight into the problems our people were facing in their everyday lives in the Canadian bush.

As soon as camp meeting was over that summer, we returned to Prince George and packed our household goods. The conference truck moved them to Mr. Basaraba's camp, where we stored our goods in the school building until we could build a house of our own. With school only two weeks ahead, we had a definite deadline to meet in getting our possessions under our own roof.

We chose a spot beside a creek just at the place where it flowed out of a small lake. The land sloped gently upward from the creek and then leveled out to make a perfect building site for our cabin. Except for some birch trees and a few Christmas-tree-sized evergreens artistically arranged on the slope, the knoll was a large expanse of grass which made a lovely natural lawn. To frame the picture, there were several tall fir trees at the back of the knoll.

Most bush cabins are built of rough lumber with no finish or paint, inside or out, and are abandoned when the timber is cut off and the sawmill is moved to another location. But we wanted a neatly constructed cabin for continued use. So we planned a structure that could be moved when desired. Thus we would not lose the money put into it.

The design was simple. There would be two sections twelve by twenty-four feet, joined together temporarily to make an L-shaped building. Separately, each section would be small enough to be hauled on a large truck. One section would be a combination living-dining room and kitchen, and the other section would be divided into two bedrooms and closets. The roof would be nearly flat, and we would use a variety of decorative plywoods to finish the cabin inside and out. And we would paint it!

First of all, we had the men at the mill saw us four large beams twenty-four feet long. These timbers, called "skids" in the language of the bush, served as the foundation for the cabin. We set them in place and blocked them up until everything was level and solid.

We obtained all the lumber that we needed from Mr. Basaraba and, when it was delivered, nailed the floor joists to the foundation of timbers and soon had the framework of our cabin well on the way up. The pastor and his family in work clothes were quite a curiosity in the lumber camp, and the fact that many came to watch, and then stayed to help, made the work go all the faster.

Occasionally we noticed someone with a practiced eye sizing things up and then expressing surprise that everything looked so plumb and square. Of course, we did make mistakes in our carpentry, but as we discovered them we tried to make the necessary corrections and thus the finished product was something we were proud of. It was no mansion, but it was the first house we could ever really call our own, and we had built it with our own hands.

With our furniture stored in the schoolhouse and the date for opening classes fast approaching, we concentrated on closing in the living-dining-kitchen section of our cabin and getting a roof on it first. We made it just in time and moved in, although there was nothing but shiplap on the outside walls and the inside still showed all the two-by-four studding and the rafters.

Next we framed up the bedrooms, closed them in with shiplap, and put the roof on. With this done, we could spread our furniture out a bit and, in a rather rugged sort of way, live quite comfortably. Now exposed to the sunlight and air, the shiplap began to dry out and shrink and it was not long until there was light showing through many cracks between the boards. This also admitted lots of fresh air, which we didn't mind at first; but by the middle of September the nights grew chilly and we were glad when the cracks were finally sealed off with building paper and the exterior finishing materials.

It wouldn't have taken us so long to get the building completed if we could have stayed right by the job. But after the first two weeks, which was our holiday time, we actually had only our spare time for the building, and sometimes I would be away from home in another part of the district for several days.

We wanted to put the plywood siding on the house and get it painted before winter set in, but by the time we got to that job it was already too cold to do any painting outside. However, by moving the furniture out of the unfinished living room, we were able to turn that part of the house into a workshop. There we pre-painted all of the siding, then took it out piece by piece and nailed it on. In this way we accomplished our plan in spite of the weather, and when the outside was finished we turned our attention to the inside of the cabin.

One job that had delayed us was the construction of a shed for storing sawdust. When we first came north we had noticed that nearly everyone who lived in the bush burned sawdust for fuel. There were two good reasons for this. First of all, it was the cheapest fuel available, for there were mountains of it around every sawmill, and all it cost was the effort of going to haul it away. There was no sawing or splitting to do—it was ready to be used as it came. Secondly, a properly adjusted sawdust-burning stove with good fir sawdust for fuel is a real modern marvel in a rustic setting.

Almost any ordinary wood-and-coal-burning cookstove can be converted into a sawdust range by taking the grates out of the firebox and replacing them with a layer of firebricks, then cutting a hole about eight by ten inches in the end of the stove. Over this opening is fastened an ingenious contrivance called the sawdust burner. On top of the burner is a large funnel-shaped hopper to hold the sawdust, which automatically feeds itself into the stove as fast as it will burn. The rate of consumption of fuel and consequently the amount of heat the stove develops is regulated very easily by simply opening or closing a draft damper on the burner to the desired position.

The result is a much more even heat than ordinary firewood could give, which makes it possible to do a really fine job of baking in the oven with a minimum of difficulty. The only attention the stove usually needs is to clean the ashes out of the bottom of the firebox daily and to fill the hopper with sawdust as often as needed. As long as the hopper contains fuel the fire never goes out, and the flame can be turned down to a mere smoldering flicker. Thus the fire could be shut down after supper was prepared and then, in the morning, started up instantly by flipping the damper open. It was as near to automation as one could expect to find in the bush!

When we set up housekeeping in our new cabin we purchased a large sawdust-burning range and installed it in the kitchen area. It had been our plan to put in an oil-burning heater also, but we never found it necessary. I built a plywood extension to the sawdust hopper, and when it was filled up the stove would burn warmly all night without any attention. When the weather turned extremely cold in the winter we could open the draft and soon the great black iron top of the stove would turn a bright cherry red and the cabin would be filled with the comfortable kind of heat that only an old-fashioned stove will produce.

The shed that we built at the back of the house would

hold three pickup truckloads of sawdust, which would last us for about three weeks in the coldest weather and, of course, much longer when the weather was mild and we were using the stove principally for cooking. Mr. Basaraba loaned us his truck for hauling the sawdust and I found that it averaged only thirty minutes of work a week to provide all the fuel we needed.

After we had built our house I made a trip in November to Lamming Mills and spent several days there. The weather had remained mild until then, but when I stepped off the train at Prince George on my way home the air was crisp with the chill of winter. By the time I had driven to Williams Lake it was 20° below zero, and I knew that something had to be done quickly to seal the inside of our cabin.

I borrowed a small truck and picked up enough Fiberglass insulation batts in town to insulate the cabin fully and then rushed home. It was just as I had expected. The shiplap and thin plywood finish on the outside of the cabin were fighting a losing battle against the bitter cold. Virginia and the girls were huddled around the red-hot range trying to keep warm, and I noticed that the thermometer in our bedroom registered below the freezing point.

We worked feverishly until late into the night and at last had the main part of the cabin insulated. With considerable gratification we felt the temperature rise until we had to turn down the draft on the stove. The next day we insulated the bedrooms and then went outside to seal the under-floor area of the cabin from the cold. This was accomplished by building a retaining wall all around the cabin. The wall was about eight inches away from the cabin and just high enough so that, when the wall was filled with sawdust, the space underneath the house was completely sealed off from the outside air.

By Christmastime we had the inside of the cabin practically finished and were snugly housed for any kind of weather. Across the creek was a fairyland grove of tiny fir trees decorated in white and sprinkled with ice crystals that glistened in the sun. Donning warm clothes and with an ax in hand we all went out together to select a Christmas tree. The ground was covered deeply with snow which, in the sub-zero temperature, made a musical squeaking sound under our boots as we tramped through the woods.

After examining the entire grove, Virginia selected just the right tree and we bore it triumphantly home, where the children, eyes shining brightly, decorated it from top to bottom. It was a real Christmas we had that year, and a happy, contented one, too, in our cabin in the bush.

There were many everyday adjustments to be made in the change from town life to living in the bush. For example, there was no running water, no plumbing, no corner grocery store, and electricity was available only when the power plant was turned on. Mr. Basaraba had a small diesel generating unit that served the buildings clustered about the little lake. There were three homes, which, together with the schoolhouse, placed quite a load on the generator; so we had to be careful not to use too much electricity at once.

The power plant was run on Mondays long enough for the ladies to do the laundry, and on Tuesdays for ironing. Otherwise we had electricity only from sunset till ten o'clock each evening. If we wished to stay up later, we used kerosene lamps for light.

Without continuous or abundant power we had to learn to get along without a lot of things we had come to take for granted in our modern world. The pop-up toaster, the waffle iron, and the electric refrigerator were stored away, and since we were often away from home in the evenings we almost forgot that we had a radio. Guests who were used to using electric shavers either struggled uneasily with safety razors or simply wore their beards.

It didn't take long to find out that most of these modern gadgets weren't absolutely essential, after all. With a little improvising here and there we provided our bush cabin with many conveniences that worked very well.

In a corner of the back porch I built an old-fashioned cooler, and we found that it kept our food fresh and cold most of the year. Our main problem with the cooler was that sometimes during the winter everything froze solid, even with the openings all closed tightly. During much of the year, any dishes that required quick chilling had only to be set outside in the snow for a short while until the desired temperature was reached.

Actually, the worst problem was the water situation. The lake water was not fit for use in the house, and the nearest source of pure water was the well in the camp cookhouse a quarter of a mile down the hill from our cabin. We purchased two five-gallon milk cans and had to carry all the water we used up the hill in the car. Everyone in the family became conscious of the problem and learned to use the precious fluid as economically as possible. On the stove we kept a ten-gallon boiler, which provided us with a supply of hot water. We also stored fifteen gallons of water in the washing machine. With the two five-gallon milk cans reserved for cold drinking water and cooking we had thirty-five gallons on hand when everything was full. Usually I had to repeat the chore of filling all the containers three times a week.

When I was away from home during the winter months, Virginia and the girls would stretch the water supply by bringing in huge tubfuls of snow and melting it on the stove.

It took eight to ten tubfuls of snow to make one tubful of water. The snow usually contained a lot of fir tree needles scattered about by the wind, which had to be strained out before the water was usable. Actually this was never a very satisfactory way of getting water. In the summer we were able to catch rain water from the cabin roof, which saved us many a trip to the well at the cookhouse.

The fact that there was no plumbing in the house meant, quite naturally, that we had to have an outside toilet. Someone from California put it this way—"We had three rooms and a *path!*" The "path" led from the rear of the cabin to a spot about fifty feet away where we erected a structure that proved to be a real conversation piece in the bush!

It was built of finished lumber (an unheard-of extravagance), closed in with plywood, and painted. It had a factory-made door, screens over the openings for ventilation, and, as its main feature, a real store-bought toilet seat. Whenever the temperature dropped below zero, a thick coating of ice crystals would form on the inside walls of the outhouse, giving it the nickname of "Crystal Palace." And there was one thing for sure—at 40° below zero there was never any problem of someone's monopolizing the bathroom!

Friends came from some distance to visit us and, after admiring our little cabin, whispered that they had heard— could they see *It?* We always obliged with pride. When, after two years in the bush, we built a house in town, we had several good bids on our luxurious version of the old-fashioned outhouse.

Even though we did not have hot and cold running water, I did install a modern two-compartment sink in the kitchen and ran a piece of plastic hose from the sink to a pit five feet deep which we had dug under the kitchen end of the cabin before beginning its construction. This made it easy for

Virginia to drain off waste water, a great improvement over
the usual bush-cabin method of putting a five-gallon pail
under the sink and then carrying it outdoors when it filled.
By this device we avoided the inconvenience of having to
empty the pail every so often, as well as the danger of for-
getting to check it and flooding the floor with dishwater.

We also tried another little innovation. In most bush
cabins washing up and bathing is done in the kitchen.
But we enclosed a small space 4 x 4 feet between the bedrooms and installed a washbasin with a drain similar to the
one attached to the kitchen sink. Equipped with two large
pitchers, one for hot and one for cold water, this little room
served its purpose very well.

Out on the back porch I made a large bin that would
hold a two- or three-day supply of fuel for the sawdust
stove, and it was the girls' job to see that this was kept full.
It wasn't a big chore, for the sawdust shed was only a few
yards away from the house; but it did mean that Virginia
never had to go out through the snow to replenish the
hopper on the stove.

When it came to buying groceries we quickly adopted the
habit of most bush dwellers. As soon as we got our pay
check we drove to town and bought a whole month's supply
of food. It took some experimenting to make this work. Since
to forget an important item meant to get along without
it until the next trip to town, we learned fast. Virginia
kept an accurate record of all groceries we purchased and
used, and finally evolved a standard list that included all
of the essentials.

Of course, we had no telephone at our bush cabin, but
we partially solved the problem of communication with
other parts of the district that had telephone service by
enlisting the aid of Brother Bob Kyte, who was in business

in Williams Lake. He kindly let his office be the clearing house for all incoming messages, which he wrote down for us. Then, every time we drove through Williams Lake, we checked in to see what calls were waiting for our attention.

I know that some city dwellers looked upon us as real martyrs "for the cause." In reality we had a lot of fun creating a comfortable way of living in the bush despite its lack of many things the city has to offer. And then there were all the things that we had that city dwellers don't usually have.

To begin with, there was the beauty of the forest itself. In the summer there were hikes to places like Desous Mountain fire lookout station, which was manned by friendly Mr. Knox of the forestry service. He always welcomed a visit from the camp children and usually had a treat of some kind waiting for them.

Mr. Knox gave me a good sermon illustration one day. We had climbed up the mountain and were listening as he explained the various pieces of equipment he used in his work. From his lofty vantage point he could look down on Mr. Basaraba's sawmill four miles away. Before our visit was over, Mr. Knox mentioned something about the mill that had puzzled him very much. He had noticed that from Friday noon until Sunday morning everything was strangely silent about the mill. There were no roaring diesel units or clattering chain saws to disturb the quiet of the forest, and he was quite curious to know the reason why. Of course, we explained to him that everyone down there observed the Bible Sabbath. It was very thought-provoking to realize that even 'way out in the bush someone miles away and unnoticed by us had been observing our lives and that what we did had made an impression upon him.

The lookout station commanded an impressive view that

took in both the coast range of mountains and the Selkirk peaks to the east. On a clear day it presented a panorama of more than two hundred miles of magnificent scenery. Closer, in the foreground, one could look down on several lovely lakes and into the wild canyon of the Fraser River.

Summertime brought a variety of delicious wild berries, which we gathered and enjoyed very much. The berries don't grow just everywhere in the bush, but as we traveled about in our district work we kept one eye open for the best places to find them. There was one big patch of wild strawberries right beside the Cariboo Highway near Clinton, and one near Bridge Lake on the way across to Little Fort. In season we could count on gathering at least a quart of berries in a few minutes and usually had a real treat by keeping them until we could reach the next town and buy a quart of ice cream to go on top.

The best wild raspberries grew on the mountain slopes back of Lamming Mills, and large, juicy huckleberries were found in abundance on a burned-over hilltop about fifteen miles north of Prince George. But the best of all were the blueberries. These little bits of delicious flavor tasted good served just about any way. Eaten fresh with ice cream, baked in a pie, or cooked and crushed to make a delicious drink, they were our favorites.

Not far from Prince George in a jack-pine forest the ground was carpeted for acres with low-lying blueberry bushes. The berries ripened in August and in a good year were really plentiful. We have gathered as many as forty quarts in one day and preserved them for use later on.

And then there were the little wild flowers. Flashing Indian paintbrushes, tall tiger lilies, delicate columbines, and the flamboyant fireweed, plus a host of other varieties, decorated the bush in profusion during the summer months.

In winter there were ice skating on the lake, toboggan-
ing and bobsledding on the hills, and informal social gather-
ings during the long evenings. Mr. Basaraba owned a sound
movie projector and showed films two evenings a month.

Wildlife was abundant all about us, and much of it could
be seen right through the windows of our own cabin. Moose
came down to the lake to drink, and to eat the succulent
water plants that grew there. Deer were plentiful. Once
a bear walked through camp, although the activities of the
loggers had chased most of these farther back into the woods.
Mallard ducks quacked and raised their ducklings on the
lake, and the woods were filled with the songs of a great
variety of birds. On moonlit nights we could hear the
coyotes howling nearby, and hundreds of frogs in the lake
gave us a solemn concert each evening. It was a symphony of
sounds and sights never to be forgotten.

All of these were what Mr. Basaraba aptly referred to as
"country conveniences," and we came to feel that they added
up to a whole lot more than all the conveniences any modern
city has to offer. When the time finally came to leave our
bush cabin for a home in town, we left with considerable
reluctance.

# 6

*~~~~~~~~~~~~~~~~~~~~~*

# WILDERNESS CREATURES

WHEN we made our first trip into the Cariboo country on the move to Prince George we quickly discovered that the northland abounds in a great variety of wildlife. It was near the close of the hunting season as we drove north, and we met car after car headed south bearing trophies of the hunt. Deer, moose, and bear were the larger animals most commonly seen. And some hunters had tracked deep enough into the wilderness to find cougar, lynx, wolves, caribou, bighorn sheep, and Rocky Mountain goats.

Sometimes visitors, hastily traveling through the Cariboo, are disappointed at not seeing many of these animals. Yet the creatures may be there just a few feet off the right of way, but completely hidden from view by the dense under-growth.

We found that we saw more game at certain times. In the summer, the best time of day is early in the morning.

Often we started our trips soon after four o'clock in the hope of seeing something interesting, and we were seldom disappointed.

During the fall, the crack of the hunter's rifle frightens most animals far away from the haunts of men. However, when the hunting season is over and the deep snows of winter make progress difficult in the forest, the larger animals frequently come out onto the roads to take advantage of the easy walking. At times we have seen as many as seventeen moose in one herd.

Late one night John Holstein and I were driving north from Williams Lake to Prince George. The snowfall that winter had been unusually heavy, and banks of white eight to ten feet high lined both sides of the road. As we rounded a sharp curve near the little settlement of Hixon, we surprised a large bull moose standing in the middle of the road. There was no room to pass him safely, and by the time the car slid to a stop we were almost upon him. The powerful beast stood there facing us and pawing the snow as though trying to make up his mind whether or not to charge.

We had heard that an angry moose could practically demolish an automobile, and we had no intention of challenging his right of way too strongly. However, after giving him several minutes to get off the road, I blew the car horn. Instead of going off into the bush, the moose turned and started walking up the road. We went after him and followed along about a hundred feet behind. But he was in no mood to hurry and, when he gave no sign of letting us pass, I stopped the car again, thinking to give him a little more room in which to maneuver his exit.

The instant we stopped, he stopped, turned around to face us, and again began to paw the snow menacingly. After watching him awhile, I turned the car lights off. This seemed to relieve the tension, and the moose turned around and started walking up the road once more. Letting him put nearly a hundred yards between us, we followed after, but the moose still gave no indication of leaving the road for the discomforts of the deep snow in the forest.

When it began to look as though we would have to travel the rest of the way to Prince George at a leisurely moose pace, we decided to close in on him. Cautiously we edged up on the great animal and then challenged him with a series of sharp blasts on the car horn. Fortunately for us, he began to run, and we pressed our advantage to the full. I shifted the car into high gear and stepped on the gas. We were soon just a few yards behind the moose who, by then, was galloping in long strides down the icy road in front of us.

Faster and faster he went until the speedometer on the car leveled off at just under thirty miles per hour. Soon great puffs of vapor from the moose's nostrils were streaming back in the cold air, and within half a mile the animal was definitely getting winded. When we decided that he had had enough, we slowed down and stopped the car once more. This time the moose took advantage of the lull in the chase and, with one mighty leap, went over the snowbank at the edge of the road and disappeared into the bush.

In many ways we found that the smaller forms of wildlife were even more fascinating than the big-game animals. The bush is dotted with numerous lakes and ponds where, as soon as the ice melts in the spring, waterfowl come to make their summer homes and raise their young. Their accuracy in timing their arrival amazed us, for often the ice would be gone from a lake for only a few hours when the first ducks flew in from the south! Since we knew almost nothing about birds when we moved into the Cariboo, we purchased a good bird book and carried it with us wherever we went. Canada geese, whistler swans, loons, grebes, ducks of many kinds, and other types of water birds moved across the field of our binoculars as we watched with intense interest the unfolding drama of wilderness wildlife.

Listening quietly from secluded places in the bush, we also discovered that the northern forest is alive with the sounds of smaller birds. Many of these stay all the year round, but most go south for the winter and return again in the spring. Besides the smaller birds, great horned owls, snowy owls, and other larger birds of prey search for food in woods and meadows, while giant ospreys with a wingspread of up to six feet and majestic bald eagles inhabit the shores of lakes and streams. Each summer the ladies at Dan Basaraba's camp ran an informal contest, for which they spent hours in the bush engaged in what they called "birding." The idea was to see who could find and identify the greatest variety of birds. Some of the lists totaled nearly two hundred.

One of the thrilling spectacles of the north is the fall salmon run. Great sockeye salmon by the tens of thousands fight their way from the Pacific Ocean into the interior of British Columbia to lay their eggs in the shallow waters of small streams far from civilization, always returning precisely to the same spot where they had been hatched.

The salmon that spawn in the Horsefly area first travel up the Fraser River, negotiating the many rapids and the long fish ladder around Hell's Gate until, nearly four hundred and fifty miles from the ocean, they turn into the Quesnel River. Sixty miles farther on they enter Quesnel Lake, and from there go into the Horsefly River, where they finally lay their eggs and then die near the headwaters of that stream. By the time they reach their destination their fins and tails have usually been battered and torn to shreds on the rocks.

As the sockeye salmon approach spawning time, their bodies turn a brilliant red. We have seen them traveling in such numbers that it seemed as though a crimson tide was moving upstream. The bears have a picnic gorging themselves on the handy supply of fish.

The government maintains an experimental fish hatchery at Horsefly where several large tanks have been built near the shore of the lake. During the salmon run, men net the big fish by the hundreds and, selecting the best specimens, remove the eggs and rush them off to the hatchery where they are kept under controlled conditions until the tiny finger-lings are hatched. Until they are big enough to fend for themselves, the young salmon are kept in the tanks. Then gates are opened and they are emptied out into the lake through large pipes.

After the experiments had continued long enough for the first salmon hatched at the station to have completed their life cycle and return from the ocean to spawn, the hatchery men found the adult fish trying to get back up the pipes into the hatchery! This instinctive ability to return to the very spot of origin is one of the marvels of nature.

Any springtime visitor to the north will assure you that the two most common forms of wildlife to be found there are mosquitoes and nosee-ums. They are quite right! The Cariboo produces big mosquitoes in great swarms. From the end of spring breakup until the middle of July they are a constant menace to comfort in the bush.

I made window screens for our car so that these pests could not get at us when we stopped along the road to rest or to eat lunch. But with the end of the spring rains and the increasing warmth of midsummer most of the mosquitoes disappeared, so that picnicking or camping out in the bush, in most places, became an enjoyable experience.

The nosee-ums get their name quite naturally. They are a small, almost microscopic, breed of insects that wield a poisonous bite. You don't notice them until they have done their damage, and then suddenly you feel an intense burning sensation at the spot where they have attacked. Fortunately these insects, too, all but disappear toward the latter part of the summer.

To explore the wilderness in its primeval beauty beyond the roads, a boat is just about a necessity. We built a small plywood craft, which we christened "Tyn-a-Mite," bought an outboard motor, and cruised the waters of many northern lakes. Our favorites in the southern Cariboo were the Horsefly and Quesnel lakes. Both of these lay about fifty miles east of the town of Williams Lake and were accessible by gravel roads.

Horsefly Lake, thirty-seven miles long, and Quesnel Lake, nearly ninety miles long, both lead back into country seldom visited by anyone. There the wild animals still roam free and comparatively safe from the hunter's gun.

Once we were camping on a sandy beach up the north arm of Quesnel Lake when I was awakened just after dawn by a "Plop, plop, plop" in the water. It sounded very much like a moose walking slowly through shallow water, but when I looked out from the confines of my sleeping bag, I could see nothing unusual. Lying down again, I heard the sound repeated a few moments later. This time I spotted a curious beaver swimming around the stern of our boat. He was splashing his broad tail on the water, perhaps in an endeavor to awaken this strange creature that had invaded his domain.

Thoroughly aroused by now, I dressed and followed the sandy shore while the beaver swam along about fifty feet away. He was in no hurry so we got a good look at one another, and I'm not sure who was the more interested, he or I. A hundred yards or so from camp I stopped and let the beaver enjoy the rest of his morning swim by himself. After watching him until he disappeared from view, I turned back toward the boat. Just then Virginia, who had been observing the scene from camp, motioned to me to look back. At the spot where I had stood a moment before, three graceful deer had stepped out of the bush and were standing at the edge of the water, breathing in the beauty of the approaching day. This was a part of the thrill of the north!

We have never carried a gun or a fishing rod, and we hunt only in order to observe the wildlife in its natural habitat. There have been those who have warned us that we are foolish to go into the bush unarmed, but we have yet to be molested by any wild animal, although we have frequently been at fairly close quarters with big game. We have found that, if we don't molest them, try to challenge their right to a trail, or corner them, most animals will leave us strictly alone. In fact, their instinctive fear of man usually leads them to run away much faster than we would wish.

Quite often, as we drive along some bush road with our boat in tow, people will flag us down to ask if we have found a place where the fishing is good. It's always amusing to us to observe the puzzled looks that come over their faces when we tell them that we've seen lots of fish but don't really know if the fishing is good or not! Some of them act as though they think we are just a little bit crazy to be out in the bush with a boat for any other purpose than to catch a trout.

But we would rather just watch the fish, with bodies glistening in the sun, leap high and free out of the water for insects. Or, perhaps, on a glassy-smooth lake we would choose to wait motionless in the boat while observing the beautiful creatures swimming in the clear depths below us.

Actually, we saw and enjoyed lots of things that the fishermen usually didn't. One day we hailed a couple of men fishing from a small boat and asked them if they knew of the whereabouts of the beginning of a trapper's trail we were looking for. They couldn't give us much information about the trail, but, in the course of the conversation, deplored the poor luck they had been having with their fishing and asked what success we had been having.

I gave our usual explanation about being vegetarians and that, since we wouldn't eat the fish, we didn't see much sense in catching them. A queer look came over the face of one of the men and then he inquired rather sarcastically, "Been catching any good *vegetables* out here?"

Fortunately, just before meeting them, we had discovered a large patch of blueberries along the lakeshore and had stopped to enjoy a real feast of them before continuing on our way. The fisherman had never thought of that possibility and, when I told him about our find, felt a bit deflated and admitted that maybe our luck had been better than his!

We hold no brief against the person who fishes or hunts for food or warm clothing, but ever since the day our family of mallard ducks were left torn and bleeding on the shore of the little lake beside our bush cabin we can't muster a high regard for hunters who shoot just for the "sport" of killing.

I say "our" ducks because we had watched that pair of birds sail in with the first flight from the south soon after spring had broken up the ice. They swam round and round the lake, quacking to each other in gleeful enjoyment at being back in the north again. Then came the family of ducklings, and daily we watched them grow. As the fluffy down turned to feathers, the parent birds taught their young to swim and later to fly and dive. By the end of summer the lake was a noisy place with all the playful quacking and the whirring of young wings being tested for the flight south that would soon be forced upon them by the cold. It was the best entertainment that we could ask for.

That fall, the hunting season opened on a Sabbath and we left for church in the morning with apprehensive thoughts about whether or not our friends would survive the day. Since the lumber camp was located on government land, we had no right to post any "No Hunting" signs, and so we had to leave the friendly birds in the hands of fate.

Returning from the services in town, we found the lake strangely quiet. At first we hoped that some inner warning had caused the ducks to flee away on strong wings before it was too late. But, walking around to the other side of the lake, the children found them.

Our mallard ducks were all dead!

# 7

## AZURE LAKE

IT TOOK misfortune to introduce us to Wells Gray Park and Azure Lake. We were on our way from Williams Lake up the Blue River Road to Lamming Mills during the summer of 1957 when a tire blew out. Previous trouble had reduced our stock of spare tires to one decrepit circle of rubber that didn't look as though it stood a chance of surviving the rest of the journey. But we put it on the car and slowly drove in to Clearwater Station, the nearest settlement on the railway. From there I telephoned to the city of Kamloops and ordered a new tire sent up on the next train.

When I had completed the telephone call it was late in the afternoon and we began to look for a place to set up our camp to await the arrival of the new tire. Then we noticed that the road leading into Wells Gray Provincial Park began right at Clearwater Station. So we decided that if we drove very slowly our bad tire might carry us into the park for the night. Proceeding at no more than ten or fifteen miles per hour over the rough gravel road, we soon found ourselves heading north into a wild, untamed wilderness of boulders, brush, forest, and mountains.

After climbing for several miles, we came out into the open and found ourselves at the rim of a deep, narrow valley through which the Clearwater River formed a ribbon of white foam hundreds of feet below. As we followed the rim of the valley farther north, the magnificent scenery of the park began to unfold before us. Eventually turning away from the river, we drove into a dense forest where the road narrowed down to snake its way among huge cedar trees. In many places the rank growth of brush and vines reached out from both sides of the road to touch the car.

About twenty-five miles from Clearwater Station we detected the increasing roar of cascading water and soon came to a marker indicating the trail to Dawson Falls. We parked our car and walked but a short distance to come out on the brink of a cliff some two hundred feet above the Murtle River. Not far upstream the river plunged over a miniature Niagara to flow on toward its confluence with the Clearwater.

Returning to our car, we drove on another mile and found a suitable campsite for the night. The next morning we discovered a sign pointing out a trail along the river's edge leading to Helmcken Falls and decided to hike down and see what it was like. The trail is a little over three miles long, but a considerable distance before reaching its end we could hear the falls. However, there was nothing about the river itself or the forest that suggested the scene that lay ahead. Glimpses of the river through the brush showed it flowing swiftly but smoothly, and the surrounding hills rose in gentle slopes.

It was certain that the trail was little used, because fallen trees, tall ferns, and tangled brush almost closed it off in many places. Pulling these aside, we forced our way through. Pushing through one last bit of brush, we suddenly found ourselves standing on the edge of a precipice. Fearfully I backed away and instinctively we all clasped hands to keep from falling into the abyss below.

A few yards to the right of us the entire Murtle River funneled through a narrow channel in the rock and then, shooting out into space, dropped four hundred and fifty feet to the bottom of a gaping hole cut out of the mountainside. The river was flowing with the full flood of melting snows from the higher mountains, and the earth seemed to tremble from the impact of the water against the rocks at the bottom of the falls. Gusts of wind were swirling clouds of mist up from the gorge until, at times, the main body of the water was hidden completely from sight. After that first breath-taking view, we scrambled along the rim of the canyon for some distance enjoying the scene from various angles.

An hour and a half later we were back in our car and headed north again. Through more dense forest, past two small lakes, down and across Lone Spoon Creek, then up and down several steep hills we went and at last came to the end of the road at a rustic cabin owned by a hunter's guide. We were forty-five miles from Clearwater Station.

From the cabin we could see the Clearwater River, flowing from the south end of Clearwater Lake, and, after a swift and dangerous passage of about two hundred yards, tumbling down low falls. Here was a good place to launch our boat for entering the lake, if we could manage to buck the current. If we should fail we would be swept downstream to certain death.

We introduced ourselves to the guide at the cabin and asked about the country farther north. He told us that after passing through Clearwater Lake, we could reach Azure Lake by negotiating a river with rapids, provided we had a powerful motor. From the description he gave us of the scenery there we decided that we should plan to make the trip as soon as we could find the time.

It was not until two years later, in the summer of 1959, that we had the chance to get back into Wells Gray Park. During the preceding winter we had spent our spare time, whenever it was warm enough, out in the shed behind the house building a new and bigger boat. This one was fifteen feet long with a beam of over six feet, and it could easily carry all the camping gear needed on an extended trip into the wilderness. We selected a twenty-horsepower Mercury outboard engine for power and equipped it with a heavy-duty propeller.

Immediately after the summer camp-meeting conference we stowed our tent, cots, sleeping bags, several boxes of groceries, and eighteen gallons of gasoline in the boat, loaded it onto a trailer, and headed for the cabin on the Clearwater River.

At the end of the road we launched the boat in the quiet water at the river's edge. After parking the car in a safe spot, I started the outboard motor in order to let it get thoroughly warmed up for the dash up the river above the falls, and then shifted the load about to get the boat in proper trim. Before casting off, I tied a stout rope through the ring on the bow of the boat and fastened an anchor to the other end of the line. Placing the anchor where it would be easy to reach if needed, I let go from the shore, pushed the throttle forward, and turned the boat upstream.

A few moments later we were safely in the quiet waters

of Clearwater Lake and sailing easily north. We found
the lake to be about a mile wide in most places, with frequent sandy beaches along the shore. It had been noon
when we left the falls; so we chose a beautiful beach and
stopped to eat lunch. Then we continued our cruise. On the
east side, the mountains became more and more rugged until
they merged into the Pilpil range, which pointed jagged
peaks into the sky far above timber line.

Halfway up the lake Mount Buchanan, ten thousand feet
high, came into view. With its snow-capped top, this mountain dominated the scenery until closer mountains cut it
off from our view.

As we continued northward through Clearwater Lake,
the afternoon sun, shining down through a bright blue
sky and drifting white clouds, warmed the landscape until
our thoughts turned to the possibility of a good swim. Near
the north end of the lake we pulled in at a beach, changed
to bathing suits, and plunged into the water. It was refresh-
ingly cool—in fact, it was so cold that we didn't stay in for
long. But we did enjoy the brief stimulation.

Sixteen miles from the falls the lake ended in a wide,
curving bay. Scanning the shoreline through the binoculars,
I could see on our left a turbulence in the water caused by
the entrance of the upper Clearwater River. We headed into
the middle of this stream and were soon sailing through
swift but smooth-flowing waters about two hundred feet
wide. I kept a sharp lookout for rocks as I set the throttle
forward in order to maintain our speed.

According to the map, we had less than two miles of
river to negotiate, but with the higher altitude of Azure
Lake, as shown on the map, we knew that there was some
rough going ahead. Everything went well until, a little over
a mile upstream, where the river made a sharp bend, we ran

into water that was flowing downstream at a very fast rate.

As the full force of the swift current struck the boat it brought our progress to a halt until I pushed the throttle wide open, and then we began to make headway again. Now the river was much narrower, so that in order to avoid the rocks along the edges we had to stay in the swift main course of water. We picked out objects on shore to watch in order to check our progress. Sometimes we noticed that we were almost standing still in spite of the fact that the outboard motor was thrashing the water as hard as it could.

After several bends, the river broadened out and we could see that, for the most part, it was very shallow. White riffles indicated barely submerged rocks, while the main part of the stream raced through a very narrow channel on the left side. In this channel the boat was only holding its own against the current. When I changed course into the shallower water to the right the current caught the side of the boat and diverted it faster than I had intended. In an instant the propeller was on the rocks. To save it from further damage I quickly shut the motor off.

As soon as we had drifted back into deep water, I jumped to the back of the boat to start the motor again. Whirling around out of control in the current, the boat headed for a large log snagged on the rocks. Virginia grabbed an oar and fended us off that, and a second or two later we were back in the main course of the river. I yanked the starter rope and, to my great relief, the motor responded with a roar and brought the boat back under control just in time to save us from being dashed on the rocks along the opposite shore.

Now slowly and with utmost caution I nosed the boat over again to the right until we could see that we were moving upstream. After safely working our way past this place, we found that the hardest part was behind us and we began to sail more easily. Soon we came to a fork in the river and left the Clearwater to turn into a tributary that took us east into Azure Lake. Free at last from the river, I slowed the motor down to a fast idle and checked my watch. The outboard had been operating at full throttle for forty minutes in order to cover the last half mile. During that time, according to the map, we had gained twenty feet in altitude.

Before us lay a scene of indescribable beauty—a lake of crystal-clear water reflecting the color of sky and clouds, bounded on both shores by forests of cedar, and dominated by Mount Huntle on the north and Azure Mountain on the south. After traveling about five miles east, we came to a wide, sandy beach on a point that jutted out into the lake. It looked like an ideal place to set up our camp; so we circled in to shore. The sand was white and clean and so free from rocks that, after unloading our gear from the boat, I had to go half a mile along the shore before I found stones large enough to use in building a campfire cooking place.

As we set foot on the beach we discovered that the sand was crisscrossed with animal tracks telling us that, sooner or later, we would have visitors. After dinner the next day I took a pan and walked along the lake shore to where a creek cascaded down the mountainside, scooped up some sand, and washed it out to see if, by any chance, it contained some gold. My disappointment was not keen at finding nothing more valuable than some flecks of gleaming mica, and I continued the process purely for the relaxation it afforded.

Half an hour later Kathy rushed up the shore from camp, beckoning me to come. I quickly emptied the last bit of sand from my pan and ran after her, wondering as to the cause of her excitement. Back at our sandy beach, she pointed out three animals swimming in the water. Apparently they had started from the opposite shore of the lake and had not noticed our camp until they were almost across. Then, wary of the scent of man, they had turned about.

We picked up the camera bag, pushed our boat out into the water, and jumped in. A moment later we had caught up with the animals, who proved to be caribou—two full-grown ones and a calf. As we came alongside of them the calf climbed up on the back of its mother and the two larger animals quickened their stroke. Swimming strongly, they soon splashed through the shallow water at the far shore of the lake and then disappeared into the forest, but not before we had taken several pictures of them. The caribou is a large animal about the size of a moose, seldom found except in the remotest parts of the bush. We had never seen one before in the wild, and it was a real thrill to be able to get such a close view of three of these magnificent creatures together.

On Sabbath morning we climbed to the top of a nearby waterfall, where we studied the Sabbath school lesson and read from the *Junior Guide* and *Youth's Instructor* that we had brought along on the trip for that purpose. It was a beautiful place for Sabbath school, and we enjoyed to the full the inspiration of the surrounding scenes of nature.

The next day we took the boat and explored the full length of Azure Lake, which we found to be about fifteen miles long. Many streams of water emptied into the lake and, besides numerous smaller ones more or less hidden under the foliage of the forest, we counted nearly a dozen large streams that tumbled down the rocky mountain slopes in white cascades and waterfalls. The largest of these, near the east end of the lake, was Angushorne Creek, which ended in a spectacular display marked on our map as "Rainbow Falls."

Evening at our campsite was a delightful time of day. As the coolness of night approached we built a large bonfire and sat about the blaze enjoying the warmth and the pleasant aroma of the burning cedar logs. Regular evening visitors were two loons and a lone grebe that sailed serenely by in search of food. Once, farther up the lake shore, we watched through the binoculars as a family of fourteen ducks went out for a swim. Other visitors passed by during the hours of the night and it was usually our first interest in the morning to look for tracks in the sand and try to identify them. Among those that called at our sandy beach were deer, caribou, coyote, and moose.

The only human visitors we had were two forest rangers who made a patrol through the area once a week. They stopped by the afternoon we set up camp and told about the surrounding country. Our map indicated some trails leading off into the mountains, and we were particularly interested in the one to Hobson Lake. The rangers described the trail as one "ten feet above the ground," an expression that was new to us. We should have found out exactly what they meant, but let the opportunity go by without further inquiry. And a few days later we started out for Hobson Lake.

Packing a lunch, we left camp at ten thirty in the morning, guiding our craft back to the west end of Azure Lake and down its outlet to the confluence with Clearwater River. There we beached our boat on the west shore, where a tiny sand bar gave us a safe landing. Mooring the boat with three lines to trees on the bank, we took our lunch and headed into the bush. According to our map, we estimated the distance to Hobson Lake to be about six miles. The trail, we thought, would be parallel to the river and some distance from it.

After covering but a short distance we came to a fairly distinct trail, where we set up a marker to indicate the position of the boat. The trail we now followed had evidently been little used, if at all, by anything except wild animals and led us in a meandering fashion around rocks, across creeks, and along the edges of swamps.

Overhead, the sunlight filtered down through the dense foliage of cedar trees in an eerie twilight glow, while underfoot the sound of our walking was muffled in a deep cushion of moss. The rotting hulks of fallen trees lay in a confused pattern here and there, and occasionally we came across the scattered bones of animals no doubt killed by cougars or wolves. Approximately two miles from where we had left the boat we came to Lickskillet Creek, which flowed along the bottom of a deep gully.

We ranged up the rim of the gully looking for a suitable place to cross the creek and in doing so discovered that some of the trees had been blazed. Immediately we realized that this was the real trail that we should have been on from the start. Following the marked trees, we found the going much faster, for we did not have to spend so much time endeavoring to keep our bearings.

However, we began to understand what the rangers had meant about a trail "ten feet above the ground." The marks were spaced from twenty-five to a hundred feet apart, and had been made by trappers traveling through on snowshoes during the winter. Thus there was no smooth path on which to walk; we had to scramble over fallen trees and around boulders in order to keep on course.

By midafternoon we knew that the hike was taking us longer than we had thought it would. At four o'clock we still had not reached Hobson Lake. Four hours earlier we had left the boat; four more hours would be required to return. After that there would be only a half hour until sunset. So, though Hobson Lake was surely no more than a mile away, we had to turn back.

The blazes leading south were not nearly so clear as the ones leading north, and before long we were having trouble in finding the way. Several times Virginia and the girls waited by the last marked tree while I circled about within calling distance searching for another marked tree. The going was extremely slow, and time slipped rapidly by. And then we reached a point where I could not find the next blazed tree.

Although we were not actually lost, we began to have some feelings of anxiety about getting out of the forest before darkness came upon us. Striking out in a general southerly direction, we had two landmarks to guide us—Mount Huntle, whose majestic summit we could occasionally glimpse through the tops of the trees to the east, and the river, which told us that we were walking in the right direction as long as we could hear the sound of its waters.

At about six o'clock we sensed that the roar of the river had faded away into the background and the forest was quiet except for the chattering of the birds. We were too far west, but when we tried to turn back in the direction of the river, we were confronted with a large, lakelike swamp, and it took us nearly an hour to work our way around it.

When we reached the far edge, to our happy surprise we found ourselves back on the blazed trail. The sun had now dropped behind the western hills and its rays were fast receding up toward the top of Mount Huntle.

We were getting rather tired by now, although we quickened our pace from marker to marker, all the time searching for the place to turn down the slope to our boat on the river.

But somehow in the lengthening shadows of evening we missed it. I knew that just downstream from the boat the river took a wide sweep to the east away from the trail we were following. Thus the farther south we went, the more difficult it would be to find our boat, which was our only means of getting back to camp.

On the hike north earlier in the day I had carefully studied the contour of Mount Huntle and when I was positive that we were already at a point downstream from the boat, we stopped to consider what we should do. It was eight o'clock—less than thirty minutes before sunset. We had forty-five minutes, at the most, before the darkness of night would set in. We could no longer hear the river and our main problem was that every time we tried to turn toward it we found swamps in the way.

Realizing that now we had no time to spare for a move in the wrong direction, we paused a moment and asked God to guide us safely to the river before nightfall. Deciding that we must go directly east regardless of the obstacles, we plunged into a tangled jungle of bushes, vines, and fallen, moss-covered trees. Soon we were at the edge of a swampy creek.

I hesitated a moment, but Kathy spoke up and said, "Let's go right through it!"

So we waded in, shoes and all, and struggled through oozing mud halfway up to our knees. Patches of giant devil's-club taller than we were flourished in the dampness and their nettles stung our hands and legs as we forced our way through. Huge ferns had to be trampled underfoot, and we all had our turn at slipping and falling over hidden rocks.

Between the swamps we ran into thick stands of alder bushes which were so dense that we practically walked over them rather than through them, although our legs were constantly falling through between the branches, making us feel as though we had been caught in a trap. By eight thirty we could hear the river again, and, fifteen minutes later, we pushed aside the last bit of obstructing brush and stood at the water's edge.

We searched the darkening landscape up and down the river to gain our bearings and came to the conclusion that our boat was actually not far upstream from where we were standing. The rest would have been easy if there had been even a small open space along the river, but the alder bushes grew right out over the edge of the bank and at that point the river was far too deep and swift for wading. However, we were so thankful that we had made it to the river that, even though it was now dark, we enthusiastically tackled the bushes and headed up along the shore. Not daring to get away from the river in the darkness, we had to watch our steps carefully. Several times I fell through the alder branches and slipped down into the river. So we quickly learned not to take a step forward without first getting a firm hold on a branch to protect us from the possibility of being swept downstream.

Fortunately, a full moon came over the mountaintops just after nine o'clock and gave us considerable light. Whenever I could, I leaned out over the bank endeavoring to get a glimpse of the boat. With only a few minutes of rest, we fought our way on until ten o'clock. Then, at last, I saw the stern of the boat less than fifty feet ahead. The river looked shallower at that point and, clasping hands, the four of us jumped into the water and waded the rest of the way.

What a welcome sight that boat was! It had taken us nearly an hour and a half of exhausting effort to work our way along less than four hundred yards of riverbank. Somewhere along that final stretch Kathy had asked, "What do we do when we reach the boat? Collapse?" That was just about how we all felt. But with grateful hearts we gathered beside the boat and thanked God for leading us safely along.

Wading through the clean, icy water of the river had refreshed us, and we quickly untied the boat. After we pushed it out into water deep enough for us to operate the motor, Kathy held the boat from being swept out into the current while I started the engine. We let it run for several minutes until it was purring smoothly.

Then Kathy climbed aboard and we were on our way back to Azure Lake. In the darkness we could not see the depth of the river, but holding an oar down in the water on each side of the boat to warn us of submerged rocks, we moved upstream slowly to avoid damaging the propeller. We reached the still waters of the lake without mishap and sailed along a shimmering path of moonlight until we arrived at our camp thirty minutes later.

The next afternoon we were resting, endeavoring to recover from the strenuous exercise of the day before, when we heard the sound of a motorboat. Through the binoculars we saw the forest ranger stop at the beach across the lake from us. He stayed there for some time, then suddenly jumped into his boat and sped across the lake to our camp.

When he came near enough, he shouted, "Do you want to see some grizzly bears?"

Of course we did! He motioned us to follow him back across the lake.

Just behind our camp, the lower part of Mount Huntle was heavily timbered; then above the timber were some grassy slopes, topped by bare rocks and snow on the peak. The grassy slopes could be seen only from the opposite shore of the lake. From that position we watched for an hour through our binoculars as a mother bear and her cub lazily walked along in the grass and finally disappeared into the timber below.

Having previously discovered blueberries growing profusely on that side of the lake, we stayed until we had filled a large pail with the delicious fruit. These we packed carefully in layers of moss from the forest floor; eventually we carried them all the way home, where Virginia preserved them in jars for the winter. Blueberry pies would surely taste good for Christmas dinner!

The next morning we were up early, for we had to break camp and get back to civilization. Soon after sunrise the boat was loaded and we were on our way down Azure Lake. Cautiously we slipped into Clearwater River with just enough power on to give us some control over the direction of the boat, but the current swept us rapidly downstream into the lake below. In just a few minutes we covered the distance that it had taken us forty minutes to travel at full throttle on the way up!

Back in Clearwater Lake I handed the controls over to Kathy, made myself comfortable in the stern of the boat, and, facing north, watched the receding beauty of the mountains among which we had camped. Before we reached the falls where we had left our car, we had the map out and were already plotting another holiday trip into lakes still more remote and perhaps even more beautiful than the Clearwater and Azure lakes had proved to be.

At least there was Hobson Lake, and the next time we would come prepared to go all the way!

# 8

## WINTER

THERE is no subtle, quiet change from summer to winter in the northland such as there is in more southerly climes. The long, warm days of July and August fly swiftly by and then, quite abruptly and almost without warning, one awakens to find that the warmth has been replaced during the hours of the night by the chill air of autumn. After that, there remain but a few days of waiting until the first snow of winter blankets the forests and meadows with a covering of white.

The brisk, cold air quickly turns the leaves of the poplars and birches to gold and orange and red, and for a brief while the hills and valleys are a riot of dazzling color. It is nature's last fling before Jack Frost takes over completely.

Winter brings a great many changes. Warm clothing is brought out of storage, and the bright hues of sweaters, scarves, and woolen caps contrast pleasingly with the white of the snow. Fur-lined boots, warm coats, ear muffs, and heavy mittens all serve to protect the wearer as the mercury falls down, down, down—perhaps to 50° below zero. Lawn mowers and garden tools are put away and huge snow shovels are placed within handy reach. Large amounts of wood or sawdust are accumulated to use as fuel. Storm windows and doors are installed, and every crack and opening is sealed against the penetrating cold.

A northern winter can be cruel to the man who is not prepared for it. But with a snug, warm cabin, plenty of good, substantial food stored in the pantry, and suitable clothing, winter is far from an unhappy time. It is, among other things, a time when scenes of exquisite beauty are arranged in almost every nook and corner of the bush. There is usually very little wind in the Cariboo and the snow piles high on fence posts, stumps, and telephone wires until the countryside looks like a patch of giant mushrooms decorated with lace. Icicles, forming on the eaves of the houses, glisten and sparkle in the sun, and the trees are all decorated as though anticipating the coming Christmas season.

Toboggans, bobsleds, and hockey sticks reappear, and the gleeful shouts of boys and girls ring through the woods as snow and ice bring again the invigorating sports of cold weather. During the two winters we lived in our little bush cabin beside the lake, Kathleen and Carolynn became good skaters and spent much of their leisure time gliding swiftly over the ice. Every time it snowed the youngsters had to shovel the snow off the ice, and sometimes it seemed that they spent more time shoveling than skating; but it was all good, healthful exercise and it didn't take much of it to turn cheeks rosy red and make appetites ravenous.

For several weeks one winter the snow conditions were nearly perfect for bobsledding. The bobsled run began at the sawmill a mile above our cabin, went past our place, and continued down the hill through the main camp and then on to a meadow below. Altogether it was a good two miles to the bottom of the hill. On the steeper parts an expertly guided sled would carry six to eight riders along at nearly fifty miles per hour. It always looked like fun as the screaming youngsters whished past our cabin; so, when they invited me to go for a ride, I gladly accepted.

At the top of the hill we climbed aboard, someone gave us a hefty push, and away we went. It was almost like being shot out of a gun, as we sped down the first steep slope, the wind whistling past my ears and the cold stinging my eyes until the tears came. But there was no getting off or stopping—until, rocketing around a curve at close to forty miles an hour, a front runner on the sled struck a hump in the ice and the driver lost control. Careening wildly from side to side, we crashed a second or two later into a bank of snow at the edge of the road. No one was hurt, but, with legs and arms still interlocked from our riding position, we were packed so tightly into the snow that it was some time before anyone could wriggle free. Snow had got into just about everything—pockets, boots, eyes, ears, and mouths, and down the necks of jackets and sweaters. But after each one had retrieved himself and shaken out the snow, we had a good laugh and went back up the hill to try it again.

However, the snow and ice and cold do present real problems. One bitterly cold night a young man by the name of John Smith rapped at the door of our bush cabin. The kitchen range he had in his house was not sufficient to keep his family warm and he was seeking help to install a heater in a bedroom.

Gathering up some tools, I went with him and we began by cutting the necessary openings for the chimney, which was to be a section of ordinary black stovepipe. After we had finished cutting through the ceiling, I crawled into the attic and began making the opening in the roof.

Brother Smith got a ladder and gingerly climbed up the slippery roof to nail down the flashing around the protruding pipe. He found it very difficult to maintain his footing on the steep-pitched roof, but he managed to get up to the peak and take a position at the peak with his body on one side and his legs over the other side. By the time the job was done, his hands were numb with the cold.

As he started cautiously to wriggle over the ridge of the roof and down to the ladder I heard a sudden "whosh" overhead, and in a split second realized that he was sliding down out of control. Aided by the light shining out of a window below, I looked through the openings between the rafters and caught a fleeting glimpse of his hurtling figure as he sailed headfirst, past the eave and out into space. There was a soft thud from below, and then all was silent.

Alarmed, I clambered down from the attic as rapidly as I could and dashed outside, calling his name as I went. Rounding the corner of the cabin, I heard a faint and muffled voice respond from the depths of a four-foot snowdrift, and then slowly a ghostly white figure emerged.

The poor fellow couldn't see a thing and could hardly talk or breathe because his eyes and nose and mouth were packed solidly with snow, but in a few moments I had him swept and cleaned off and Brother Smith, much to my relief, assured me that he was not hurt. We had a good laugh over the dramatic finale to our evening's work and went inside to try out the new stove. It worked fine.

While deep snow can certainly cushion the impact of a fall or, perhaps, save a car from damage when skidding off the road, it can also cause some annoying experiences. One

Sabbath morning we started out from Dan Basaraba's lumber camp to go to church at Beaver Valley. A deep layer of fresh snow had fallen in the night and the road crews had had no chance to clear it off with their huge plows. We had little difficulty in traveling the sixty miles to our destination, but the front of our car did considerable "plowing" on its own and kicked up a lot of snow along the way. But we thought nothing of it.

After the church service was over, I went to start our car, but the engine wouldn't so much as turn over. Not even the starter would move. Puzzled, I raised the hood to see what was wrong. To my surprise, I found the entire engine sheathed in ice. Apparently a large quantity of snow had been thrown up under the hood, and while the car was parked the warmth of the engine had melted the snow, which had then frozen again into a coating of solid ice. The men from the camp got a blowtorch from the mill shop and, after heating the engine with the torch, gave a tow with another vehicle until the car started.

By far our most serious transportation problem in wintertime was getting the car started when the temperature ranged below zero. At zero degrees Fahrenheit a car battery puts out only about half of its normal power and, as the temperature drops down still further, so does the efficiency of the battery. This, combined with the increasing stiffness of the engine lubricants, can make it very difficult to start an engine in extreme cold.

Good electric engine warmers are available but, since we had no constant source of electric power at our bush cabin, we had to rely on keeping our car in top mechanical condition. We usually started the winter out with a new one, for we found that we could often do our best work when the weather was the coldest. The sawmills shut down when it was 20° below zero because their machinery does not function properly at colder temperatures, and the people were generally at home then. Thus we tried to keep mobile regardless of the weather.

When the mercury stood at 30° below, or colder, I never let the car stand idle for more than two or three hours at a time. Thus it was necessary for me to rise at intervals through the night, don an overcoat, and go out to run the engine for fifteen to twenty minutes.

The ability of an automobile to withstand the abuse of cold always amazed me. At 45° below zero a cold engine fairly screams as it first turns over, and it takes a fair amount of time before any oil pressure shows up on the dashboard gauge. Brakes freeze fast, gears are next to impossible to shift, and the steering wheel is almost immovable. Often I had to let the engine warm up for ten to fifteen minutes before it would develop enough power to put the car into motion.

Before the days of tubeless tires we had frequent trouble with inner tubes. Extreme cold made the rubber so brittle that the tubes would crack. Sometimes doors and windows could not be opened because they were sealed shut with ice. I discovered that a frozen lock could usually be thawed out by inserting into the keyhole a key that had been pre-heated by a match. We always had good heaters installed in our cars, but sometimes it was so cold that a bottle of drinking water carried inside the car would freeze solid as we traveled along.

Getting stuck in the snow was another problem. We will never forget the time we got stuck nine times in one day. After a fresh fall of snow Virginia and I set out on a wintry day to make calls in Beaver Valley. The road at that time was so narrow in most places that, even in summer when the surface was dry, two vehicles meeting each other could pass only with caution.

Now the snow was piled high on both sides of the road and there was not enough room for a truck and a car to pass. Soon we met a truck and had to resort to the usual procedure. Since a heavily loaded lumber truck does not dare leave the road, the car driver purposely turns off as far as possible into the deep snowdrifts beside the road. Then the truck pulls by, and the driver brings out a chain carried for the purpose, hooks it onto the rear of the car, and pulls it back onto the road. The system works, but is terribly inconvenient. It is not unusual to have to go through this experience once or twice on a trip to Beaver Valley, but on the day in question we went through it five times.

After making several calls at the lumber camp, we started down the valley to the home of Mrs. Long and her son Kent, where we had an appointment for a Bible study. On the way there we met another car. This was different from meeting a truck, for it was highly doubtful if either car would have enough traction to pull the other out of the ditch. Both of us moved as far as possible to our respective sides of the road and, after a bit of jockeying about, the other car pulled safely past.

But when I tried to proceed, the rear wheels of my car would only spin, although I was firmly on the road at a level place. I got out to see what was the cause of the trouble, feeling quite puzzled at being stuck under such circumstances with no apparent obstruction in the way.

The trouble was that the slight warmth in the tires had begun to melt the ice during the pause, reducing traction. The spinning wheels only served to make a deeper depression. We had to do some energetic pushing before we were on our way again.

A few moments later we were driving across the Longs' farm. Near the house the road crossed a low bridge over a small creek. In order to make it up the other side, I had to approach the bridge with considerable speed. Just as we started across, a ridge of ice caught the front wheels and turned us sharply off course. Although there was no railing on the bridge, a bank of heavy snow stopped us with only one wheel over the edge. We left the car as it was and walked the rest of the way to the house for the Bible study. After that, Kent Long came back with us to help shovel snow away from the car. Then, with Virginia at the wheel, Kent and I pushed the car back onto the bridge.

That evening we stayed for prayer meeting in Beaver Valley and about nine o'clock started for Dan Basaraba's camp, where we were living at the time. Sixty miles on icy mountain road go by rather slowly and it was nearly midnight before we turned off onto the Basaraba mill road. More snow had been falling, so that in order to get up the hill to camp, I stopped to put on the tire chains.

A mile from home the snow became so deep that we stalled right on the road. As I repeatedly backed up and lunged ahead the radiator water started to boil. When I checked, I found the fluid level so low that I decided I had better walk up to the house and get some more antifreeze mixture for the cooling system. By the time I had reached home I was so exhausted that I was wishing for a ride back to the car. To my joy, I found Brother Basaraba's four-wheel-drive power wagon parked nearby. He had invited me to use it whenever necessary; so I walked over to see if, by any chance, the key was in the ignition switch. It was, and I happily drove it back down the hill to where Viriginia was waiting in the car.

After adding the antifreeze to the radiator I decided to

tow the car with the power wagon. Since there was no room to turn it around I hooked a chain from the front of the truck to the front of the car and began to back up with the car in tow. Everything would probably have gone well if I had been able to see the road behind the truck a little better. But before I could realize what was happening, the truck swerved, skidded into the ditch beside the road, and was half-buried in deep snow drifts.

Even with the four-wheel drive engaged the wagon would not budge. There was nothing to do but get the shovel and dig it free from the snow. By the time I had moved enough snow to accomplish that, there was sufficient room in which to turn the truck around and we were soon home. It was two o'clock in the morning and another day was finished.

In spite of the difficulties, we thrived in the cold weather. Winter brought us many good times, and we often remarked about the fun we had and how we would miss the cold weather if we ever had to move south again. We thoroughly enjoyed the challenge of a wintry blast from the arctic regions, and I determined that no hazard of weather or road would keep me from meeting appointments. With only a very few exceptions, I was able to hold to this program.

At first some people were a bit surprised to see us arrive at times, but it didn't take them long to learn our habits. One Sabbath morning we drove up to the Beaver Valley church with the outside temperature nearly 50° below zero. Inside the building, the people had gathered for worship and the chapel was comfortably warm. The deacons were busily engaged in feeding great slabs of wood into a red-hot furnace made out of a fifty-gallon oil drum, and told me, between armloads, that they had been busy all night with the job.

I found out that on Friday evening people in the camp had nearly decided to cancel the Sabbath services on account of the cold. The local elder had reminded them that it was my Sabbath to visit them and suggested that they should go ahead as usual. So they had divided the deacons into shifts to keep the fire roaring all through the night in order to have the building warm in time for Sabbath school. Needless to say, I appreciated their efforts to please me—and was glad that I hadn't disappointed them. In spite of the cold outside, we had a wonderful time enjoying fellowship together that day.

We know it was not determination alone that enabled us to carry on our work through the winter months. I always felt that God commissioned special angels to watch over us as we traveled along the icy roads and that many times we arrived safely at our destination only in answer to prayer.

One particularly cold night I had to drive up a steep grade near Williams Lake. Although several sharp turns on the hill made it impossible to maintain much speed, I usually got up this stretch of road without much trouble. But that night the hill was sheathed with glare ice and, when I had proceeded but a short way, the wheels lost traction and began to slip and spin.

I half backed and half slid the car down to the bottom of the hill and took another run at it, but to no avail. When that failed, I knew that the tire chains had to be put on. I had no trouble laying out the chains, backing the car over them, and bringing the ends into position to be hooked. But I couldn't fasten the hooks without removing my gloves. When I took my gloves off, my fingers stuck to the cold steel. Again and again I tried to fasten the hooks, but I couldn't do it.

When my fingers became so numb with the cold that they

felt like useless sticks I sat in the car for a while and warmed them by the heater. Intense pain throbbed through my hands as the circulation was restored. Then I tried again to fasten the chains. After several unsuccessful attempts, I gave up.

When I finally decided that there was nothing more that I could do, I sat in the car and asked God to get me up that hill if He wanted me to meet my appointment. After prayer, I put the chains back in the trunk of the car, and was about to back down the hill again and give the Lord the advantage of a head start when I decided that, if the Lord wanted me to get up that hill, He could do it just as easily from where the car stood. So, shifting into low gear, I carefully engaged the clutch. The wheels gained traction at once, and the car moved up and over the top of the hill. The angels seemed very close that night.

I'm sure that Kathleen will never forget the day of her baptism—for more reasons than one! Following a series of evangelistic meetings held in the Prince George church, a group of ten persons, including Kathleen, had requested baptism and we happily proceeded with the arrangements. The church members at Prince George had installed a fine baptistry in their church but had not yet been able to afford the installation of a system to heat the water.

We decided that we could solve this problem by filling the baptistry about two thirds full with cold water and then warming it by the addition of hot water brought in milk cans on Sabbath morning from the homes of several of our church members. Although it was December and well into wintertime, the weather had remained mild, with outdoor temperatures above zero. So Friday afternoon, after putting the cold water in the baptistry, we stoked and dampered the furnace in the church and went home.

Sabbath morning we awoke to find that a front of arctic air had suddenly moved south during the night and that it was 45° below zero outside. We hastily dressed and went to the church, where we found things just as we had feared. It was freezing cold inside and a thick layer of ice covered the water in the baptistry. With the help of the deacons, we fired up the furance and soon had a roaring blaze going, but the building never really warmed up that day.

Then we made the rounds of the homes of our church members and brought all the hot water we could get. But when the last canful had been poured into the baptistry, the ice had barely melted. However, every candidate was there for the service and no one wanted to postpone the occasion.

I think that we had an unusual service that day. We had heard of our ministers breaking the ice to hold outdoor baptisms during the winter, but never had we heard of anyone breaking the ice to conduct an indoor baptism! But hearts were warm and glowing with the love of God and it was a day of rejoicing for all of us.

# 9

## BEAVER VALLEY

ODT and Harold Jacobson were born with saw-milling in their blood. Their great-grandfather had built and operated a lumber mill in Norway before the middle of the nineteenth century, and the boys' father, Arnt Jacobson, was carrying on at the same establishment fifty years later. When Arnt Jacobson migrated to the New World at the turn of the century he tried several different ways of making a living, but always his first love was for the timber.

The year 1927 found Mr. Jacobson farming near Edmonton, Alberta. But when Ed Chesley, a total stranger, wrote a glowing letter to him promoting the development of a lumber business in the northwestern part of British Columbia, he was interested. The next year Mr. Jacobson went by train along the route from Prince George to Prince Rupert and selected fifty acres of heavily timbered crown land on the bank of the Shames River about fifteen miles west of the little town of Terrace.

The property was covered with huge cedar, spruce, and hemlock trees. Dad Jacobson felled some of these trees to make a clearing near the railway track, which bordered his land on one side, and then built a small cabin. After this was completed, he returned to Alberta, rented his farm, and took his family west. When the train stopped in the bush to let the Jacobsons out at the site of their new home it was with some misgivings that mother Jacobson herded her brood of growing children off into the wilderness.

There were three boys in the family, Alf, Odt, and Harold, and two girls, Alice and Ethel. The first thing they noticed as they got off the train was what seemed to them to be the biggest pile of brush they had ever seen. In the clearing, several acres in extent, the trees lay just as they had fallen. Branches in great profusion pointed skyward at grotesque angles to give a starkly desolate appearance to the scene and, out in the middle of all this tangle of logs and branches, in lonely isolation, stood a little shack twelve by eighteen feet.

Mrs. Jacobson questioningly turned to her husband and asked, "Where are we going to live?"

He replied by pointing to the shack and saying, "Over there."

With real courage Mrs. Jacobson made a home for her family in that crude shelter of rough boards. The comforts of life were extremely limited. At night the children climbed a ladder through a hole in the ceiling and crawled back between the ceiling and the rafters of the cabin to sleep. The next summer Arvid was born, and then there were eight in the family.

Dad Jacobson and a crew of hired men set to work to build the sawmill. They located it beside the Shames River, where they built a water wheel and took advantage of the natural source of power to operate the machinery of the mill. By the time the Jacobsons were in business the family savings were depleted, but the future looked bright. Once the mill was sawing logs into lumber everything would be all right.

But, just as they were ready to go to work, the great financial depression struck and these pioneers found themselves struggling against the poverty of the "hungry thirties." With their money all invested in the mill, the Jacobsons could not have moved elsewhere if they had wanted to. All they could do was to fall back on their own courage and resourcefulness, and they needed every bit they possessed in order to pull through. On the farm in Alberta they had at least had a garden, plenty of grain, a cow, and some chickens. Here they had nothing but the forest.

The children scoured the countryside for wild berries, a task which they found rather frightening at times, for the woods abounded in bears who wanted the berries as badly as they did! But, despite the competition, the children brought in quantities of blueberries, red and yellow salmonberries, and huckleberries, which helped to fill empty stomachs. The boys fished along the Shames River, and, although the Jacobsons did not ordinarily use meat, when they had to they shot wild game to keep themselves in food.

The Jacobsons had accepted the Seventh-day Adventist faith when they were farming on the prairies and now, no matter how isolated they were from other believers, or how difficult the times, they faithfully adhered to the message that they had embraced. Even though they spent many Sabbaths alone, they always had Sabbath school and endeavored to give their children a solid spiritual training. God rewarded them in many providential experiences through those hard years of the early 1930's.

Notwithstanding every effort, once during that first rugged

winter of the depression the family faced a bare cupboard. There was nothing left to eat, and no money to buy any groceries. But God was watching over them. Just at the time of their greatest need Mr. Jacobson received a letter from a man he had never heard of before—nor has heard of since. This gentleman requested him to look at some property in the nearby town of Terrace and give him an appraisal of its worth. There was a $10 bill enclosed for his trouble. With a thankful heart for God's providence, Mr. Jacobson hurried off to Terrace, took care of the business for the man, and then spent the money for groceries.

After the mill had been in production for a while, life for the Jacobsons took a turn for the better, even though the price of lumber was very low. They made railroad ties for the Canadian National Railway, and before long their income was such that they were able to build a more comfortable home for themselves. They also purchased a cow and some chickens and, as they cleared the land, were able to grow all of the vegetables they needed.

At first they used a team of horses to bring the logs to the mill, but the time came when the horses were replaced by a model-T Ford truck. And so, little by little, the ruggedness of the first years in the bush gave way to a more settled manner of life.

But the Shames River never let them fully relax their struggle against the wilderness. Since they depended upon the river for power, the mill always had to be close to the riverbank. This would have been all right if the Shames had been a docile stream. But heavy rainstorms swelled it into a wild, uncontrollable torrent of water that frequently changed its course in a few hours.

During one of its rampages, the flooding stream swept away almost everything they had—barn, livestock, chickens, and tool shed—as well as threatening to undermine and destroy both their home and the mill. The Jacobsons hastily moved into another cabin half a mile away to escape the river. But they had barely settled in their new home when another rainstorm lashed the area and the family awakened in the night to the ominous, terrifying roar of crashing timber. The river was moving again and, by morning, had completely changed its course, flooding right past the new house. They quickly gathered up their possessions and moved back to the old place, which now stood high and dry. As the boys look back at the Shames River days it seems to them that their main battle was with the river—either it was chasing them across the property, or they were chasing it for power to run their mill!

In the early days at the Shames River site there were no roads in that part of the country. Nothing cut through the wilderness except the railroad and a few blazed foot trails. In order to get into town for mail and supplies the Jacobsons bought a hand-pumped rail car and obtained permission from the railway to use the track. Later on, when they could afford it, they bought a rail car called a "speeder" which was driven by a small gasoline engine, and they used this machine extensively to get from one place to another.

This was not without danger. One evening Harold started out to the post office and store on business for the family. Speeding along the track, he was rounding a curve in a narrow cut when he was suddenly confronted by an unscheduled fast-moving freight train. There was no time to stop— only to jump. Without so much as touching the brake on the speeder, Harold leaped off to the side and, just as he rolled to a stop in a pile of rocks, the cowcatcher on the locomotive rammed the speeder and demolished it into bits of flying debris. Fortunately Harold picked himself up unhurt, but he had to pay for repairing the damaged cow-catcher—and he had to walk home from the scene of the accident.

As the Jacobson boys grew up, they developed into resourceful, hard-working men, and, though present prosperity has eased the hardships of those pioneer days, they realize that the move to Shames River gave them a background of experience that few young people today have the privilege of receiving. The parents believed in Christian education and sacrificed to send their children away to school. Alf, the oldest son, went on to the College of Medical Evangelists and returned to practice medicine in British Columbia. As the children left home to obtain their formal training for life, the family, one by one, scattered, and finally dad and mother Jacobson retired to a comfortable home in the Okanagan Valley a few miles south of the city of Vernon, British Columbia.

However, Odt and Harold stayed by the sawmill business. In partnership with two friends, George and Delmer Reiswig, they selected a spot at China Valley, north of Vernon, and set up a mill. After four years of successful partnership with the Reiswigs, the men decided to sell their business. Following this, the two Jacobson brothers heard of a promising section of timber near the little village of Horsefly, forty-five miles east of Williams Lake in the Cariboo country. Another company had been working the place until their mill had burned down and the loss had forced them out of business.

After investigation, the brothers decided to buy the timber rights and venture out on their own. Friends tried to dissuade them by pointing out that they were going into a wilderness with an uncertain future. But the same pioneering blood that had sent dad Jacobson to the Shames River urged them on, and they went ahead with the plan to move into the Cariboo.

The remnants of a camp still remained at the site of the burned-down mill, which was situated at the head of beautiful Beaver Valley, seven miles from the village of Horsefly. The first two men to arrive at the camp to begin the work of reconstruction were Harold Jacobson and the company's truck driver, John Stickle. They brought up a truck-load of equipment and pulled into the valley just after dark one evening early in December of 1954. Odt Jacobson and his wife Rosy arrived a few hours later.

The camp had a deserted, desolate appearance. The cabins were nothing but poor shacks surrounding the charred and blackened ruins of the old mill. The men looked the cabins over and picked out the best one as a place in which to spend the night. There was no electricity, no furniture, no glass in the windows. It was cold, and they were tired. For a brief moment Odt and Harold wondered if, after all, this coming to the Cariboo country had been the wisest thing to do!

Almost as soon as they arrived, snow began to fall heavily, and Harold asked his truck driver to pull the truck into a garage that they had noticed across the camp. Then they set up beds and retired for the night. During the darkness the snow continued to fall, and by morning everything was buried under a fresh white blanket. When the men went out to begin work they discovered that the building in which they had parked the truck, to protect their equipment from the storm, had no roof. In the darkness of the evening before they had not noticed that fact and now, in spite of their precautions, the load was smothered in snow.

It didn't take long to get things in order and, when the rest of the crew arrived a few days later, the families cheerfully faced the discomforts of the rough camp while the men enthusiastically worked to put into operation a temporary mill, which they used through that first winter. Later, the Jacobson brothers put up a permanent building and installed modern machinery for sawing the logs and for planing the rough lumber. For the forty-five-mile haul to the railway at Williams Lake they purchased a big tandem White truck, which is capable of carrying twenty thousand board feet of lumber each trip.

Today the annual production of Jacobson Brothers Forest Products, Ltd., averages eight million board feet of finished lumber, or enough framing material to build more than a thousand new homes every year. The company employs approximately thirty men, most of whom are Seventh-day Adventists.

The Beaver Valley church was officially organized in the camp soon after the crew and their families arrived, and it has been very gratifying to watch the impact of this group on the people of the surrounding area. Sabbath afternoons find church members driving their cars into the village of Horsefly or walking down backwoods trails to distribute literature bearing the message of Christ's return to earth.

While many whom they met at first had never heard of Seventh-day Adventists, it was amazing to discover how far the third angel's message had already penetrated into the bush. An elderly lady, found living in a little house by the side of an isolated lake, was asked if she belonged to any church. "Oh, yes," she replied, "I belong to the Voice of Prophecy." With age confining her most of the time to her lonely home, she had listened on her battery-powered radio to the Voice of Prophecy broadcast, and it meant so much to her that she considered it her church.

Businessmen who call at the mill are frequently led to

comment on the unusual nature of the crew, so different from the rough, unkempt, and swearing men so often found in the lumber camps. Some have had special opportunities to discover the amazing honesty of the workmen. A mechanical engineer representing a machinery company in Quesnel came to install a new carriage in the mill. When the job had been completed, he picked up his tools and returned to Quesnel, only to discover that he had left a good fifty-foot steel measuring tape behind.

"Well, you'll never see that again," his employer told him. But, several weeks later, when the engineer returned to check the performance of the new equipment, he found the tape measure just where he had left it.

Experiences like this impressed all who heard about them, and the community soon realized that these Adventists were distinctive in other ways than the observance of the Seventh-day Sabbath. Even the good behavior of the children drew favorable comment from visitors to the camp.

The honesty of the men at the mill had a large part in leading Mrs. Long and her son Kent to join the Seventh-day Adventist Church. Neighbors of the Jacobsons, the Longs raised beef cattle on a ranch about four miles down Beaver Valley from the lumber camp. Occasionally, when an extra man was needed, Kent filled in for a few days at the mill. One time he forgot to take his heavy apron home with him and was very much surprised to find it unused and waiting for him when he was called back to work again a few weeks later. Although he had known very little about Adventists before meeting the Jacobsons and their crew, his interest was now aroused to find out more about their beliefs.

The Longs had moved into the Cariboo country in 1950. The previous years had been spent on cattle ranches in Wyoming and Montana until their adventuresome spirit led them to launch out still farther to the north. They chose British Columbia as the most likely area and then wrote to several newspapers published in the province requesting their listings of cattle ranches for sale.

One advertisement that appealed very strongly to them was for a three-hundred-acre tract of land along Beaver Creek in the Cariboo country. It had a house described as "strictly modern and newly redecorated," and the price was modest. After arranging to purchase the property, the Longs moved into the Canadian bush and worked hard to build up the ranch.

There were some disappointments. For instance, the "strictly modern" house proved to be a rambling log structure with a kitchen sink as its only claim to modernity! But Mrs. Long made it attractive and homelike, and the lovely view of the valley helped to compensate for the lack of conveniences.

But the hardships took their toll, and slowly it became evident that Mr. Long was failing in health. During the winter of 1956 he underwent surgery, which seemed only to aggravate the trouble. Early that next summer, Verna Jacobson, Harold's wife, visited the Longs, who were impressed by her kindly interest in their problems. It was this kindness which later led Mrs. Long to call on Mrs. Jacobson for advice about her sick husband.

Verna said, "I'll call Harold. He has very good judgment and will know what to do."

Mr. Jacobson suggested that the Longs go to Burnaby, near Vancouver, where his brother Alf had his medical offices. When it became evident that the Longs weren't fully prepared at the time to meet the expense involved, the Jacobsons purchased round-trip bus tickets to Burnaby for them. Although the Longs were able, later on, to reimburse the Jacobsons for this expense, the kindness was never forgotten.

On this trip they learned that Mr. Long's troubles were further complicated by diabetes, and it seemed that no successful treatment could be found for his combination of diseases. He was in and out of the local hospital a number of times after returning to the ranch. Then he suddenly became very ill in the early spring of 1957 and was sent to a specialist in Vancouver. Three weeks later he was gone.

Bravely Mrs. Long returned to the Beaver Valley ranch and carried on. Her son Kent stayed with her, and today the two work side by side caring for their cattle.

Through the months of anxiety and trouble, a close friendship developed between Mrs. Long and Verna Jacobson. Invitations to attend special services at the camp church were accepted and, little by little, Mrs. Long and Kent learned more about the beliefs of their neighbors. They read such books as *The Desire of Ages*, *The Great Controversy*, and *God Speaks to Modern Man*, and then began to study the Bible earnestly. Others from the camp took a friendly interest in the Longs and encouraged them in their study.

Through the winter of 1957-1958 Virginia and I had the privilege of visiting regularly at the ranch, and the Longs gladly accepted the truths of God's word. By summertime Kent and his mother had made their decision to unite with the church. We walked down the grassy hillside to a deep pool in Beaver Creek where, in the beautiful setting of their own ranch, they were baptized.

Others, too, who live among the hills surrounding Beaver Valley are pondering the witness of the members of the lumber-camp church. I am sure that as they watch and study, others will come to a similar decision and there will be more of these picturesque ceremonies.

# 10

## DEDICATED TO GOD

W‌HEN dad Lamming gathered his sons about him to give them his parting advice, he took a matchstick and, while they silently watched, broke it. Following that he took several matchsticks together and tried to break them, but without success.

Then he said, "Boys, if you'll stick together nothing can break you!"

Three of the boys—Gordon, Oscar, and Ernie—have pretty well followed that advice through the years, and what their father predicted has held true. Dad Lamming started them in business early by organizing the family farm and a small sawmill near Sault Sainte Marie, Ontario, into a company with himself and the boys as partners.

The three sons, now men of mature years and experience, live together in an Adventist community called Lamming Mills, the center of a large lumber and farm development carved by courage and toil out of the rugged Canadian wilderness near the headwaters of the mighty Fraser River. Their story is a thrilling account of dedication and adventure.

In the early 1920's the brothers decided to move to Port Alberni on Vancouver Island, British Columbia. They tried various business ventures, most of which were mildly successful, and eventually got into the freight business.

In 1928 a timid Seventh-day Adventist lady called at the home of one of the Lammings and asked for a Harvest Ingathering donation for missions. She was so impressed with their generous gift—$2—that when Elder H. L. Wood was sent to Port Alberni to preach the advent message, she made a special point of inviting the Lammings to the meetings.

They were interested and, as they listened to Elder Wood's preaching, came under the strong conviction that they ought to unite with the Sabbathkeeping church.

The fact that their trucking business involved the regular delivery of fresh foodstuffs to many of their customers on Friday evenings and Saturdays presented a real problem to the brothers. As they thought it through, they felt that, if they were going to follow their consciences regarding the Sabbath, they would have to sell out and get into some other line of work. It would not be fair to ask their customers to accept the inconvenience that would be caused by this new-found faith. It was not easy to give up a successful enterprise such as theirs.

Their decision for God was made in the summer of 1931, three years after they had first heard of Seventh-day Adventists. This was no halfhearted surrender to their Lord. From the moment their decision was made, these men were dedicated heart and soul to God. The later development of Vancouver Island and the Port Alberni area indicates that, if the brothers had chosen instead to stay with their trucking business, they would now be millionaires. But there is no trace of regret.

In choosing a new enterprise, the Lammings were motivated by the thought that there must be many Adventists who faced Sabbath problems. They decided that their business must be the means of providing work for as many Adventist brethren as possible.

For two years after becoming Seventh-day Adventists the brothers operated a coal mine in Alberta. Then came a proposition that was to affect their lives and the lives of many others for years to come. In 1934 the Lammings contracted to log off a million feet of timber near Rocky Mountain House, Alberta. They stayed at Rocky Mountain House for nine years until, as timber became scarce there, they began to look for another location. Then the brothers heard that a man who owned some timber rights at McBride, on the British Columbia side of the Rockies, had lost his mill by fire and wanted to sell his timber.

As they investigated this stand of timber the Lammings were impressed by vast areas of virgin forest growing along the banks of the Fraser River. On either side of the river the mountains rose until the trees became stunted and then vanished in the thin, cold air of the snow-swept summits.

There was no doubt that they had found enough timber to last them for years, but most of it was considered inaccessible. The district forestry officer warned the brothers that they would never get the timber off the steep slopes and vowed he would eat his hat if they succeeded. But in spite of the forbidding obstacles, these pioneering spirits decided to move west across the Rocky Mountains.

It was no small undertaking. There were five freight-car loads of logging and mill machinery, miscellaneous equipment, and household furniture for several families, plus a carload of horses, to be moved across the mountains by rail.

Oscar and Ernie Lamming with their families and the mill crews filled seven automobiles, which started west in caravan style over the rather primitive roads.

All went well until the party left Jasper and began the climb through Yellowhead Pass. It was in the spring of the year and the road, which had been closed to traffic in the winter, had not yet been cleared of the rocks and debris left by avalanches and melting snow. Just out of Jasper they were confronted by a padlocked chain across the road.

What should they do? With all of their possessions going on ahead of them by train they could hardly turn back now. Not wishing to break the padlock, the men carefully examined the barrier and discovered that one post to which the chain was fastened was loose. So they lifted it out of the ground and carried both the post and chain to one side of the road. After driving the cars past, they replaced the barrier and the caravan rolled on.

Crawling over the summit, the party soon found itself in great danger on the steep grades and sharp curves of a road that was really nothing more than a mountain trail. One car developed brake trouble and careened down the hills unable to stop. A car driven by Dave Quering overturned, but, just as Ernie Lamming was about to give orders to halt the trip before anyone was killed, the caravan arrived in less hazardous territory and was able to continue without further difficulty to the little frontier community of McBride, which was the rail terminal to which their goods had been shipped.

The arrival of the caravan was the most exciting event the valley had ever experienced. Seven cars! These, exactly doubling the number of automobiles in the district, and the quantity of freight and horses, were the topic of conversation in every lonely log cabin up and down the river for miles. The town of McBride felt the impact so strongly that it soon erected its first stop sign in order to help control the increased traffic.

For the first two years the men worked with a portable mill, which they moved from place to place as they cut the timber. Skill combined with hard labor and determination developed the business to the place where the Lammings were able to plan the erection of a permanent sawmill and camp for the employees.

They chose a level piece of land just above the Canadian National Railway track about seven miles west of McBride. There they laid out a little town of several streets and built their homes, a church, a school, a store, and a post office. The sawmill and a planing mill were located on the west side of the new village with a covered chute connecting the mill with a spur track on the railway. When everything was completed, the finished lumber could be loaded directly into freight cars waiting on the siding.

Logging roads were bulldozed through the bush and up the steep slopes of the mountains, and roaring "cats" and powerful diesel trucks replaced the horses that had at first brought the fallen trees to the portable mill. The timber that the forestry men had warned could never be brought out of the bush began to pile up like giant matchsticks in the mill yard. There the logs waited to be pushed into the mill pond and started on their way to becoming the framework of homes across Canada and the United States.

Those logging roads always intrigue me, as does the daring of the men who bulldoze them out and drive trucks over them. Whenever I could take the time I walked over to the mill pond and hitched a ride back into the mountains with one of the men. Mile after mile the huge truck crawled

up one steep hill after another. Although the upgrade climb
was made empty, much of it required shifting down into
compound low with the four-wheel drive engaged. Finally
reaching an altitude which offered an eagle's-eye view of the
valley below, the truck stopped at a clearing where the
"cat" drivers were pushing or dragging the logs into a load-
ing area. There a man, operating a machine called the
jammer, lifted the logs onto the truck. When the load was
complete, the driver cinched them down with heavy chains
for the trip to the mill.

In winter, when the logging road was covered with ice
and snow, only the large end of the log was placed in a steel
cradle mounted on the back of the truck and the rest of
the tree slid along behind on the ice. With ten to twelve
great logs, sometimes one hundred feet long, chained to the
truck the ride down the mountain was a real thriller. Once
under way, the logs gained momentum on the ice and almost
instantly it became a life-and-death race between truck
and logs to get to the bottom first. The only way to control
the course of the logs was to keep the truck ahead of them,
and the driver had to depend upon a delicate sense of
balance and sheer nerve to make a safe and successful run.
It is only on such a trip as this that one can realize how
nearly correct were the men who said it couldn't be done.

Steadily the business grew. The brothers were able to
expand, developing a fine dairy herd and farm in the McBride
valley, and entering into several lines of business in the
town. Gordon Lamming later moved into the valley and
worked to develop the farming potential of the land. He
discovered and cleared soil that produced as much as twenty-
two tons of potatoes to the acre and shipped the produce out
in carload lots.

As the years came and went, the community of Lamming

Mills took on the appearance of a settled town. The people improved and painted their homes. Children grew up and went off to college. Wedding bells rang in the village church, and older crewmen retired and stayed on in the beautiful valley.

Then came the tragic night of January 24, 1955. Sitting at home that evening, Ernie Lamming noticed that the lights in the house kept dimming and brightening, and decided to find out what was causing the trouble. Over at the mill, where a diesel engine generated electricity for the camp, he discovered that a thermostat designed to keep the oil warm in the hydraulic system that operated some of the machinery had failed to function properly. As a result the oil became overheated, burst the hose, and then ignited. When Ernie Lamming arrived, the flaming liquid was pouring out and spreading over everything.

The cry of "Fire!"—dread scourge of sawmilling—rang out on the cold winter air and quickly aroused the camp to the danger. But it was already too late. Giant flames, fed by the spreading oil, licked away at the tinder-dry beams of the mill. In a few moments it was all ablaze. Clifford Brucks, a crewman, got a "cat" going and the men threw chains around the diesel power units, which were torn loose from their mountings and dragged out of the flames. Then, just in time, the "cat" driver sent his machine crashing through the conveyor chains that moved the lumber from the saw-mill to the planer, and thus the fire was confined to the one building.

But the loss was almost overwhelming. The next morning the brothers surveyed the charred and still smoldering remains of their sawmill and pondered what they could do. Under the deep conviction that they should continue in the responsibility to which they had dedicated their lives—providing employment for Sabbathkeepers—they made their decision. If the Lord would help them, they would build again.

With courage and faith the management and crew began to plan for the future. First of all, they set up a small temporary sawmill and, by operating it for two shifts a day, kept production going. Then, drawing upon the past years of experience and the expert advice of others, the Lammings drew up plans for a new and modern mill.

By the first of December, a little over ten months after the fire, the crew shut down the temporary mill and moved into the new building. It was truly a moment of triumph in the lives of these men of faith. Today the mill, operating smoothly and efficiently, produces an average of 375 freight-car loads of finished lumber annually—more than one carload for every day in the year. With a crew of nearly 70 men, the Lamming brothers are fulfilling their dream of providing work for Sabbathkeepers.

God is abundantly prospering the business, and the community looks back upon the tragedy of the fire as a blessing in disguise because of the progress which followed it. Both the company and the employees faithfully remember that they are but stewards of the Lord's goods, and they liberally support the church's program of world evangelism. The record reveals that, since the move to the McBride valley in 1943, the church at Lamming Mills has forwarded to the conference office more than a third of a million dollars in tithes and offerings.

In addition to making these direct contributions of cash, the company has responded generously to appeals for lumber to be used in church-building projects. In Sault Sainte Marie, where the brothers grew up, there now stands a place of worship for Sabbathkeepers. The lumber for the building came from Lamming Mills, produced by men whose greatest joy is to see the cause of truth advance.

The operation of the mill itself is a witness for God in lumbering circles throughout the province. When it was completed it was hailed in the news as the most modern sawmill of its size in the interior of British Columbia. Recently the Workmen's Compensation Board of the government requested permission to make a sound motion picture of the entire setup to show throughout the lumber industry as a model of efficiency and safety.

The believers at Lamming Mills not only support the Lord's work throughout the world field, but are actively engaged in evangelizing their own valley. Through visiting in the homes of the people and establishing branch Sabbath schools they have found many opportunities to present the truths of the Bible to their neighbors. All are encouraged to take part in these home-missionary activities.

In 1946 a shy young lumberjack from the Adventist camp walked unannounced into a cabin up the valley and, without a word of explanation, placed in the hands of a man by the name of David Shelby a copy of the book *Our Lord's Return*. Awkwardly waiting awhile, the young man then turned and walked out as silently as he had entered, feeling, no doubt, that since he was too timid to talk in the presence of strangers it was actually useless for him to try to do anything for the Lord.

Having no interest in religious things, David Shelby put the book away without reading it.

Years before, when he had left home to seek his fortune in the west, David Shelby's mother had given him a Bible. Out of respect for her he had accepted it, but this Book was left in his trunk and never read. He obtained a good position with the railway out west, and the future looked bright. But life seemed to lack that elusive something the man wanted more than anything else and for which he vainly searched through the years.

In the west, David Shelby came into possession of a magnificent and beautiful Belgian stallion which for many years was his almost constant companion. Together horse and rider traveled the rugged wilderness of the upper Fraser River country, slept beside each other along the trails, and developed a close and understanding attachment one for the other. Then, in 1952, the great stallion died, and David Shelby, overcome with grief at the loss of his faithful companion, remembered the Bible his mother had given him long ago. Seeking comfort, he got it out of the old trunk and began to read.

He started with Genesis and read it all the way through to the last chapter of Revelation. Through his grief he commenced to feel the great power of the Holy Spirit working within him. The comforting message of the Bible so fascinated him that, when he had finished it once, he began to read it all over again.

There were many things that he did not understand at first, but he determined to master the truths of the Bible. As he read it through the second time, one thing, at least, became clear in his mind—the right day to keep as the Sabbath is Saturday and not Sunday.

As his interest in the Scriptures deepened, David Shelby reached out for help and accepted religious literature of various sorts. He studied the writings of the Christadelphians and of Jehovah's Witnesses, but always there was the conviction about the Sabbath that kept him from joining any specific movement. While continuing his study of the Bible, he rediscovered, one day, the discarded book that had been given him six years before by the shy young man. The message of *Our Lord's Return,* convincing him of the importance of the Sabbath truth, so thrilled David Shelby that he determined to read more literature prepared by the same publishers.

In the meantime, he became acquainted with Carl Ganz of Lamming Mills, who gave him a copy of *The Great Controversy.* By the time he had finished that book he knew what he had to do in order to make his peace with God.

Mingled with the joy of finding Bible truth was the problem of his position with the railway. He knew that he could not expect to be granted Sabbath privileges. The best that the company might do for him would be to offer him a lower position, which would mean laying off a fellow employee. He also realized that his working schedule would inconvenience many of the other men. His anxiety concerning these things kept him in the valley of decision for some time.

Then something strange and moving happened. On August 16, 1955, David Shelby, in a dream, was lying at the dawn of day on the bank of a ditch looking across a meadow. As he watched the grass waving in the breeze, he suddenly heard the rumble of thunder. Looking up, he saw great clouds, beautiful beyond description, roll across the sky. While the thunder crashed and reverberated from mountain to mountain, he gazed at the scene fascinated, until a strange light appeared in the eastern sky. The source of the light moved closer and closer, glowing more brilliantly as it approached. Then he recognized the majestic figure of Christ in a circle of blazing glory.

When he realized that Jesus was coming, great fear swept over him. He had not yet taken his stand for the Sabbath truth and now, face to face with Christ, he felt that he was lost.

David Shelby awoke from this dream feeling certain that

God had divinely warned him that he ought not to hesitate with regard to keeping the true Sabbath. Rather than cause any inconvenience to his fellow employees, or any ill feelings, he chose to resign his position with the railway and follow his Saviour all the way.

There was an outdoor baptistry just beside the Lamming Mills church, but Brother Shelby expressed his desire to be baptized in a river, exactly as Jesus had been baptized. So we found a quiet spot along the bank of the Fraser River and on a beautiful Sabbath afternoon, in company with the believers from the sawmill camp, David Shelby and I went down to the river's edge together.

He walked into the water with happy heart and peaceful mind, for he knew that he had at last found what his soul longed for. In preparation for his baptism, he had assessed the value of all of his possessions. Just as we left for the river he handed me a statement indicating that he had computed the tithe on the entire amount. This account with the Lord was settled in full a few days later. Thus David Shelby joined the long list of men and women who down through the ages have dedicated everything to God.

Soon Brother Shelby was serving the Lamming Mills church as a deacon and his faithful witness in the McBride valley gives daily evidence of what can be accomplished when a man surrenders to his God.

And so the circle of influence ever widens. What will God yet accomplish because, more than thirty years ago, a dedicated woman knocked on the door of a stranger, Mr. Lamming, to ask for an Ingathering donation?

# 11

## TO THE END OF THE ROAD

When Andy Waterman and Lorna Ratcliffe asked me to perform their wedding ceremony my adventuresome spirit soared to new heights, for the wedding was to take place at Bella Coola.

Bella Coola is at the end of the road—a thin, dotted line of ink on the map running westward three hundred miles from Williams Lake. I had often looked at that line on the map with the wish that I might be able to visit the Bella Coola valley. But there never seemed to be quite enough time to get into a place so far off the beaten track just to take a look. However, now that I had an important job to do there, the needed opportunity had arrived and I prepared for the trip with great eagerness.

Situated at the head of a long, narrow inlet of salt water coming in from the Pacific Ocean, the town of Bella Coola exists quite apart from the rest of the world. From the town, a narrow valley pierces the wilderness for a few miles to the east, where it ends at the foot of the precipitous cliffs of the Coast Mountains.

Until recently, about the only contact the valley has had with the outside world was through the weekly visit of a small coastal vessel that calls for passengers and delivers mail and supplies. But now a road has been blazed over the Coast Mountains and down to Anahim Lake to connect with the road from the interior. As yet, this has done little to disturb the quiet of the valley, for only the most intrepid tourist will venture that far into the wilderness.

We inquired around Williams Lake but could find no one who had made the trip all the way into Bella Coola. So the day before the wedding was to take place, Virginia and I started west, not knowing exactly what was ahead of us. Twelve miles from Williams Lake the road snakes down a steep grade into the Fraser River canyon. There it crosses the great river on a creaking, swaying suspension bridge barely wide enough for one vehicle at a time. The bridge spans the Fraser at a point where the powerful, surging current swirls through between massive rocks jutting out into the stream. There is a "STOP" sign at each end of the bridge and motorists are warned that only one vehicle is allowed to cross at a time, and, when the way is clear, to proceed at no more than five miles per hour.

Safely across the Fraser, we climbed steeply for eight miles until the land leveled out onto a vast plateau of rolling hills and lush grazing land known as the Chilcotin. Here rugged pioneers with ranches of fabulous acreage graze cattle by the thousands and, with the help of Indian cowboys, drive the steers to the stockyards at Williams Lake each fall for marketing.

As far as the big ranch at Tatla Lake, which is at the

midway point between Williams Lake and Bella Coola, the road is of gravel surface, fairly wide in most places, and usually passable with little difficulty. But from Tatla Lake west the road is, for the most part, not much more than a trail bulldozed through the ever-returning bush. The open range country is left behind and the scrub forest that takes its place is spotted with swamps. About the only sign of human habitation to be seen is an occasional hunting lodge or a band of roving Indians camped by some lake. The settlement at Anahim Lake is the largest community along this lonely stretch of the road and is made up of several Indian families, a Chinese trader, a schoolteacher, and a few white settlers.

The entire Chilcotin country is so sparsely inhabited that, after we had crossed the suspension bridge over the Fraser River, we met only six vehicles, most of them trucks, on the three-hundred-mile trip to Bella Coola, an average of one every fifty miles.

West of Anahim Lake the trail begins a noticeable climb into the Coast Mountains. Leveling off quite abruptly at an altitude of nearly five thousand feet, the road soon plunges without warning into a terrifying descent down sheer rock walls and steep, shifting slopes of loose gravel and boulders into the canyon of the Bella Coola River. A few trees somehow manage a foothold in places here and there. Down these precipitous cliffs the road drops nearly to sea level in just twelve and a half miles.

It is no small test of nerves to move down a ledge barely wide enough for one car, with no guard rail whatsoever, facing the fact that even a single moment of carelessness could catapult a car and its occupants to instant destruction thousands of feet below. But we reached the bottom of the canyon without mishap and proceeded into a narrow valley walled in on both sides by towering, jagged mountain peaks. In forty miles we sighted twenty glaciers and, by the time we had reached the town of Bella Coola and the end of the road, we were enthralled with the wild beauty of the country.

A hardy band of white settlers located in the valley about the turn of the century and established themselves on small farms. Their successors continue to enjoy the rich soil combined with the mild climate of the coast and the long, sunlit days of a northern summer, which produce amazing crops of vegetables to be stored away in cellars for use during the winter months. Most of the farmers have some fruit trees, a cow or two, and a few chickens. Fish from the sea, venison, moose meat, and bear brought in from hunting expeditions make the settlers almost independent of the outside world. Plenty of timber is available from which to build their homes, and firewood for warmth and cooking is to be had for the cutting and splitting.

While the loneliness of the valley has driven some away through the years, many who came into Bella Coola so long ago have never left, and they live their quiet, peaceful way, content to let the rest of the world go on its troubled course without them. About half of the valley's population of fifteen hundred people are white settlers. The rest are Indians who make their living mostly by fishing in coastal waters. Many of these families own well-equipped, powerful boats and live in comfortable homes ashore.

The wedding was performed in the little community church at Hagensborg, nine miles up the valley from Bella Coola. Having been built before electricity was available, the sanctuary was lighted only by candles which cast a soft, flickering glow over the waiting throng of relatives and friends who had come to hear Andy and Lorna exchange the vows that made them one "till death do us part."

While we were at Bella Coola we met Lorna's mother, Mrs. Frank Ratcliffe, and Lorna's grandmother, Mrs. Ida Hober. We were also introduced to Mrs. John McHardy, Lorna's aunt. These three ladies formed the nucleus of a tiny Sabbath school that gathered from week to week in the Ratcliffe home. It had been a long time since they had been visited by an Adventist pastor, and they expressed their longing for someone to come and spend awhile with them and perhaps to hold some meetings in the town.

We promised to pass their request on to the conference brethren, but nothing materialized until the following year when we were asked to go back to Bella Coola and spend a few weeks with our people there. The conference also invited Brother and Sister Clyde Gildersleeve to assist us with the meetings that we planned to conduct.

These good people, who in previous years had sold many truth-filled books in the area, left their work at the MGM Logging Camp at Smith Inlet and sailed north in their boat, the "Sea Gypsy," to be with us. Many years before, Clyde Gildersleeve's father had logged in the Bella Coola district and there still remained in the minds of the Indians the memory of a very kind Christian gentleman. This helped us to make a number of friendly and favorable contacts among them.

So it was that September of 1957 found us heading west again to the end of the road. We obtained the use of the town's little theater for three nights a week and then visited every home in the valley with an invitation to attend the services. It was difficult for many to come simply because they had no transportation; others were friendly, but hesitant about listening to anything new; but a fine group did attend the few meetings that we held.

A number of Indians came regularly and we enjoyed getting acquainted with them and visiting with them in their homes. These people had had so few privileges that they really appreciated the interest we showed in bringing the message of God's love to them.

On Sabbaths we gathered up several carloads of interested people and took them to Mrs. Ratcliffe's home for an afternoon meeting. As many as twenty-four crowded into her living room for Sabbath school and Bible study. Mr. Ratcliffe, although not a member, extended his warm, frontier hospitality to all of us and joined in with the meetings. Once the group had been brought together we usually made a day of it and followed the meeting with supper and a social evening. Often we just sat around and listened while Frank Ratcliffe regaled us with tales of the early days in the valley.

One evening, as we were listening spellbound to a spine-chilling encounter Frank had had with a grizzly bear, pandemonium suddenly broke loose in the farmyard just outside the house. The dog began to bark, chickens squawked, and cattle bellowed. The boys ran out just in time to frighten off a black bear that had come down to investigate the tantalizing aromas drifting out into the bush from a freshly slaughtered steer that was still hanging in the barn.

We had left Kathleen and Carolynn at home in Dan Basaraba's lumber camp under the care of Mr. and Mrs. Elmer Hedlund. After a few weeks away from them we decided to make a quick trip back to visit the girls and then return to the work at Bella Coola. The length of time we would have yet to spend at Bella Coola was now almost entirely dependent upon the weather. The road over the mountains was not kept open during the winter, which meant that an early snowfall would necessitate cutting the series of meet-

ings short in order to get out of the valley before the road
became impassable. But we desired to stay as long as
possible. A good interest in the meetings was developing and
we wanted to plant as many seeds of truth as we could before
leaving.

After a brief visit at home, we started out early one
morning on the long trail back to Bella Coola. It was November and there was a chill breath in the air. The leaves
on the trees, except for the evergreens, had turned gold and
orange and then had fallen. The bush stood stark and naked.
Up on the Chilcotin range country the little lakes and ponds
were fringed with ice, and, blowing up over the Coast
Mountains, fierce black clouds warned that a storm was
ahead.

As if in premonition of something worse happening farther
along the road, a tire blew out near Tatla Lake. Another few
miles and the engine began to overheat. Upon investigation,
we discovered that one of the rattles in the car was due to
the fact that the radiator had worked loose. The consequent
chafing had resulted in a serious leak in the cooling system,
so that we had to make frequent stops at ponds along the
way to add water to the radiator.

West of Tatla Lake, gasoline fumes creeping into the
car indicated that something else was wrong. Fortunately,
it was just the spare can in the trunk of the car that had
sprung a leak. We solved that problem by emptying the
remaining gasoline into the car tank.

By the time we passed the hunting lodge at Kleena
Kleene, the sky overhead was dark and foreboding. We
anticipated a snowstorm but, as the wind increased in
strength, it brought with it the milder temperatures of the
Pacific Ocean and soon great drops of rain began to spatter
the windshield of the car.

The rain settled into a steady downpour that drenched the Coast Mountains all the way to Bella Coola and soon softened the dirt surface of the road until the going became increasingly difficult. The miles went by more and more slowly, and it was not until ten o'clock at night that we reached the summit of the pass through the mountains.

Before starting the perilous descent into the Bella Coola valley, we stopped to relax for a few moments. It is surprising how much comfort the sound of a steady, dependable engine can bring under circumstances such as this, and it was not until I had turned the headlights and the ignition off that the full impact of our situation began to impress itself upon us. Now there was nothing but impenetrable darkness, the constant pelting of the rain, and the shuddering of the car as strong gusts of wind howling through the pass rocked it from side to side. We had had the road completely to ourselves for the past hundred miles, and it was all too obvious that we were very, very much alone in the wilderness and the storm, except for God.

We bowed our heads and prayed, "Dear God, we need Thy special protection just now. Even under the best of conditions, the road ahead is dangerous. We do not know what damage this storm may have done. We are endeavoring to do Thy work, and we ask Thee to guide us safely down to the valley below."

I pressed the starter button and we began the descent in low gear. However, we had not proceeded far before we realized that the storm had worked havoc with the road. Eight hours of steady rain had loosened boulders that came crashing down to strew the way with impassable obstacles. There was nothing to do but get out and remove them. Some were so heavy that we had to cut down small trees to use as levers to get them out of the way. The combination of rain and wind had uprooted trees that now lay fallen in solid barricades to block our progress. The smaller trees I cut into short lengths with the ax and we pushed them out of the way with our bare hands. Larger trees I cut into logs with the saw and then, throwing a hitch around them with the tow rope, used the car to pull them to one side.

During the twelve-and-a-half-mile descent from the summit, we had to get out into the rain twenty-four times to move rocks and seven times to move trees. Always there was the danger that more rocks and trees might come down on us any moment as we worked. By the time we reached the valley, our clothes were thoroughly soaked and we were chilled and exhausted.

As the road leveled out and we began to anticipate the comfort and warmth of our room at Bella Coola, we came to a place where a small creek ordinarily passed through a culvert under the road. Now a swollen torrent of water, the creek was flooding the road for about one hundred yards.

We stopped and calculated the risk, then proceeded slowly. Everything went all right until, about halfway through the flooded section, the right side of the car suddenly dropped into a large hole that had been scooped out by the current. The car bounced to a stop and would move no farther.

Taking off our shoes and socks and rolling up the legs of our slacks, we waded out into the stream to see what could be done about the situation. If the right side of the car, we decided, could be jacked up and some planks placed under the wheels we might just possibly make it out of the hole. With the flashlight, we began to search along the road for something that would serve the purpose. Apparently the flooded culvert had replaced a small bridge and so we located some heavy planks lying discarded beside the road. We dragged two of them back to the car and got the jack out. But as fast as I could set the jack in place, the water washed away its footing and this, together with our having to hang onto the planks to keep them from floating away, made it a losing battle.

In addition to these problems, the water was steadily rising, the floor of the car was now flooded, and our feet and legs were badly bruised and cut from the rocks that were being swept along by the current.

When our flashlight gave its last flicker and went out, we gave up and crawled back into the car to sit out, with legs curled up on the seat, the remainder of the night. The clatter of gravel and rocks rolling against the car, and the roar of the water, kept up a steady din in the darkness, but by four a.m. it stopped raining and by seven o'clock, when it was light enough to see, the water had considerably subsided. With the shovel I succeeded in diverting the stream from the road and then, without the hindrance of the water, we soon had the car jacked out of the hole and were once more on our way.

Several miles down the valley the road climbed steeply up the face of a cliff overlooking the Bella Coola River. There, rounding a sharp curve on the narrow ledge, we were suddenly confronted by a gaping hole. A large section of the road had completely disappeared into the river nearly two hundred feet below. Gingerly we backed the car off the cliff to a safer position, for this was something we could not cope with alone.

We cannot know for sure, but, as we surveyed the slide, we definitely felt that God had answered our prayer for protection by holding us fast in the clutches of that flooding stream during the final hours of the night. We could have been on the cliff when it gave way and plunged to certain death without leaving a trace of what had happened to us. With a new vision of the nature of divine providences, we thanked God for the adversities of the night. Then, leaving Virginia behind in the car, I scrambled over the rocks above the washout and set out on foot toward Bella Coola in order to obtain help.

Hours later I reached a lonely farmhouse where the people quickly responded to the situation and took me back in their car to get Virginia and then drove us to our room down the valley. I sent word to the Public Works men about the road, and then we tumbled into bed for a much-needed rest. The next day the road crew stopped and took me out with them. I watched for several hours while they closed the gap with logs and rocks until I was able to get my car safely across.

The next few days brought colder weather and fresh snow on the mountaintops. Each morning the snowline was lower until, by Sunday morning, we could see that it had dropped below the five-thousand-foot level.

I turned to Virginia and said, "Tonight must be our last meeting if we are to get over the pass before the snow is too deep. Even now it may be too late."

We spent the day visiting the ones who had been attending the meetings, encouraging them to continue their study of the Bible. There was much more that they needed to know. But now they would have to wait until someone could again come to the end of the road to teach them.

More snow fell in the mountains that night. In the morning we packed and loaded the car as quickly as possible, but it was after noon by the time the work was done and the last good-bys had been said. On both trips into Bella Coola we had brought a considerable amount of evangelistic equipment, as well as personal luggage, and now it was all crammed into one load, so that the car was riding low. Consequently, we moved slowly up the valley road, which still bore the marks of the previous week's storm. With the short days of winter upon us, it was already dark when I paused to shift the car into low gear at the foot of the steep climb out of the valley.

To make it up and around the first sharp bend in the road, I pushed the throttle to the floor and, as I did so, a terrible grinding and grating noise came from underneath the car. Not knowing what was causing the noise and fearing to stop to investigate lest I could not get the car going again on the steep grade, we drove on until the road leveled off for a few yards.

There we stopped and, with the flashlight, I crawled under the car to see if I could find what was wrong. I finally noticed a bright spot circling the drive shaft and a corresponding spot on the bottom of the car. Evidently the combination of the heavy load and the hard pulling had caused the drive shaft to rub against the floor board. Naturally, I was quite relieved to know that nothing mechanical was actually wrong.

However, as I was sliding out from under the car, the beam of the flashlight shone on the inside of a rear tire and revealed a protruding lump as big as a baseball. This was a serious problem! I had tried to replace the tire blown out on the way into Bella Coola the week before, but could not find one the correct size for my car. There was still one spare tire left, which I now put on in place of the one with the large lump. This left us with no spare tire, two hundred and fifty miles of bush road ahead of us, and an overloaded car.

Virginia and I talked the situation over and decided to

go back seven miles to the Talchako Hunting Lodge and spend the night there. At Talchako we were shown a rustic, but comfortable, room. However, before retiring for the night, I unloaded all but absolute essentials from the car and arranged for the owner of the lodge to bring the things out in his truck to Williams Lake the next summer.

Early Tuesday morning we set out again up the pass. This time there was no grinding noise under the car and we pushed steadily upward until, at about 3,500 feet, we reached the snowline. I mounted the tire chains and we went on through fresh, untracked snow that got deeper and deeper as we neared the summit.

At the last, we were proceeding by driving into the snow until it stopped us, then, backing up to take another run at it, gaining a few feet or yards with each new thrust. Three times we had to stop to let the smoking clutch cool down and, for a while, it looked as though we might not be able to reach the summit. But, after several difficult hours spent on the slippery, narrow road up the canyon walls, we were over the top.

On the other side, it was comparatively easy going downhill, even in the deep snow, and by noon we were at Anahim Lake. At Anahim Lake we stopped to eat the lunch which Virginia prepared for us in the car. Before going on, I made a careful inspection of the tires and in doing so found one front wheel almost too hot to touch. One of the men in the settlement there helped me to remove the wheel and clean the brake cylinder, which had seized from rust. This was doubtless due to the night spent in the water on the trip into Bella Coola.

Happily, we had no more trouble with the car, but it took us another day and a half to get home. From Anahim Lake down the eastern slope of the mountains a layer of mild air had moved in and melted most of the heavy snow. We plowed through a sea of mud nearly one hundred miles long until we reached firmer road near Williams Lake.

At the edge of town we stopped at Bob Kyte's office to let him know that we were back from the west and to find out if he had any messages for us.

He greeted us by asking, "Do you know that the Royal Canadian Mounted Police are looking for you?"

In answer to our rather startled looks, he explained that Elder Smithwick, the conference president, had tried to get a telephone message through to us at Bella Coola but had been told that we had just left for Williams Lake on the way out. That was Monday morning. For two days he had tried to call us at Williams Lake and when he realized that we still had not reached home, he feared the worst for us and had asked the Mounties to begin a search. This they did, but never quite caught up with us.

I phoned the police and informed them that we were safe and thanked them for their efforts in our behalf. Then I called the conference office to let them know that we were back from the end of the road.

# 12

## THE LOVE OF GOD

WE WERE not in the north for long without coming face to face with the enslaving effects of alcohol. Not that the problem is necessarily more acute there than elsewhere but, in keeping with the rugged characteristics of frontier towns, it is brought out more into the open. Men staggering down the sidewalk, bloody street fights, gaunt-faced children waiting outside in the cold while bleary-eyed mothers try to satisfy their evil thirst at the bar, hungry families, and broken homes—these are everyday scenes that scar the north with tragedy.

Sawmill owners hesitate to pay their men because they know that the money will often be spent in wild drinking sprees that leave their crews unable to work and the mills idle. Most of the men earn good wages when they work, but some never save a penny and live in abject poverty, all because they are slaves to alcohol. Losing control of their will and their self-respect, they go from bad to worse until illness, accident, or crime may close the awful chapter of their life.

But even among this group all is not hopeless. Some sense the meaning of their situation and struggle desperately against the tide that is sweeping them on to destruction. Often their struggle is all alone and against such tremendous odds that, in spite of all their efforts, they go down in final defeat. The fortunate few are the ones who place their problem in the hands of God and who have the help of understanding Christian friends.

Fred and Elvira Johnson lived in a small log cabin seven miles north of Williams Lake. Both were alcoholics, smoked heavily, and tried to get what fleeting pleasure there was in a circle of associates who cared little or nothing for God. Nights of carousal followed by days of quarreling had brought their marriage to the brink of disaster.

A few well-meaning persons, who became acquainted with the plight of the Johnsons, tried to help them, but it seemed that they had nothing but a confusion of ideas to offer. It all appeared hopeless. Mrs. Johnson, longing with all her heart to save her home, and yet bound by the tyranny of satanic power to the thing that was taking from her what little joy remained in life, could see nothing ahead but the bleakness of despair.

One morning, after a particularly bitter quarrel with her husband, Mrs. Johnson was walking across the meadow to a little creek to get some water for her housework. As she walked along the trail, she knew that she needed help and that it must come soon. The thought came to her that, if no one else could help, perhaps God could. She set her water pails down, stepped over to a secluded spot in the trees, and there on her knees she told the Lord all about her troubles and pleaded that He would send her help that day.

That afternoon there was a strange rap at the cabin door and, when Mrs. Johnson went to see who was there, a young man introduced himself as Marvin Suiter, a Christian worker. She invited him in and listened as he described the book *The Modern Medical Counselor* and appealed to her to purchase it for her home. However, when she told him that what she really needed was spiritual help more than physical help, Brother Suiter showed her a copy of *The Desire of Ages*.

As Mrs. Johnson listened to the colporteur and observed his keen interest in her spiritual welfare, the realization came to her that this visit was God's answer to her prayer. This man was not just trying to sell her a book, but he was there with a message that would help her to solve her problems.

Before the visit was over, Mrs. Johnson explained her situation to Brother Suiter, who encouraged her to continue to seek help from God and then knelt in prayer, asking the Lord to lead the Johnsons to complete victory over their alcoholism. Mrs. Johnson did not have money at the time for the book, but Brother Suiter left her a copy to read for a few days and arranged for either the book or the money to be left with a friend in Williams Lake where he could pick it up later.

Before he left her cabin, Mrs. Johnson found out that Marvin Suiter was a Seventh-day Adventist. Although she had never heard of a church by that name, she was profoundly impressed by the fact that, when she had asked God for help, He had sent an Adventist colporteur to her aid.

Mrs. Johnson began reading *The Desire of Ages* and spent hours studying it with ever-deepening interest. The beautiful story of Jesus and His love touched her heart and began to take effect in her life. Now the word of God meant more to her than it ever had before. She enrolled in the Twentieth Century Bible Correspondence Course and read another book, *The Great Controversy*, which Brother Suiter left with her on a later visit.

In contrast to his wife's enthusiasm, Fred Johnson was not interested in what these unheard-of Adventists had to teach. He had been brought up in another faith and, although he made no pretense of living up to it, felt that his baptism as an infant was all the religion he needed.

Near the close of the year 1954 Elder M. L. Long, a retired Adventist minister living in the southern part of British Columbia, heard of the Johnsons and felt impressed to visit them. In December he drove north to Williams Lake and from there out into the bush where Mr. Johnson was helping to operate a small sawmill. Ordinarily, Mr. Johnson would have been too busy to spend much time with Elder Long but, quite providentially, the Caterpillar tractor that brought the logs to the mill broke down just before the pastor arrived. It took three days for the owner to get the parts and make the necessary repairs. During that time the mill was idle and Mr. Johnson had nothing to do but to listen to what Elder Long had to say.

Elder Long arrived on Friday afternoon and began to study the Bible with the Johnsons that evening after supper. They studied until late into the night, then retired to sleep for a few hours. As soon as breakfast was over the next morning, the Bible was brought out again and studied until lunchtime. After lunch, they continued until supper, and then far into the night again. Mr. and Mrs. Johnson were hearing things that they had never heard about before, and the revelation of God's love and the plan for man's redemption held them spellbound. Fred was now just as much interested as his wife had been before. They carefully questioned Elder Long, and then proceeded as each point was made clear.

On Monday noon, after almost three days of continuous Bible study, Elder Long left to return to his home. The repairs on the tractor had been completed and Fred Johnson went back to work, but not before they had had time to study every major Bible doctrine. Now both Fred and Elvira were fully convinced that they had found the truth. Now they had something to live for, and new hope filled their hearts. Friendly letters from other Adventists who had heard of them brought encouragement, and the Johnsons began their battle against alcoholism in earnest.

Early in February of 1955, just a few weeks after we had arrived in the Cariboo country, Brother Suiter told me about the Johnsons, and Virginia and I went to visit them. We found that they had moved to a rough bush cabin five miles off the highway. It was nighttime when we went to call, and we drove cautiously between high banks of snow along a narrow, winding, and unfamiliar road until we saw a light flickering in the distance. The light came from the Johnson home, where we were warmly welcomed and encouraged by the progress that they seemed to be making. Their great desire was to prepare as soon as possible for baptism and membership in the Seventh-day Adventist Church.

A few weeks later, when I was again in the Williams Lake area, I called on the Johnsons. This time it was during spring breakup and I was unable to drive my car all the way to their home. So I parked the car when I reached an impassable stretch of mud and walked the remaining three miles. When the cabin door was opened in response to my knock, a nearly empty liquor bottle on the kitchen table silently told a tragic story of defeat.

An atmosphere of discouragement and gloom pervaded

the Johnson home and, with hearts filled with remorse and hopelessness, they told me of the battle lost to the old enemy. They felt that it was useless for anyone to try to help them any more.

Although I tried to encourage them to try again, in my own heart I felt as helpless as they did. I knew that, if the Johnsons ever gained the victory over this enslaving habit, it would be nothing but a miracle of the love and power of God. The only thing left to do was to earnestly seek the working of this miracle that was so much needed in their lives.

As I trudged back through the melting snow and the mud to my car I wondered if the effort to help these folk would come to nought. But I was not ready to give up yet. Since the Johnsons' companions were nearly all people who lived for this world and who encouraged the thing that they were fighting against, I felt that some earnest, understanding Christian friends would bring them added strength to help in overcoming temptation.

Among those who responded to the need were Odt and Rosy Jacobson of Beaver Valley. They called on the Johnsons, and, as they saw the problem the Johnsons faced in their struggle against alcohol, the Jacobsons decided to see what they could do to meet the situation in a practical way. With this in mind, they invited Mr. Johnson to work in their mill at Beaver Valley. So it was that the Johnsons moved to Beaver Valley in the early summer of 1955. There, surrounded by Adventist neighbors, they made rapid progress spiritually.

But it was not all easy. Necessary trips to town for groceries and other supplies brought them in touch with old associates and sometimes the temptation to drink seemed too great and the long-established habit overwhelmed them.

But, in spite of the defeats, there were more and more victories. As the Johnsons experienced the joy of real living again, they sought with ever-increasing determination to be forever free from the world. God rewarded their determination and, after a time of severe testing, altogether removed the taste for alcohol.

The battle against tobacco was almost harder than that against intoxicating drink. Fred Johnson had smoked for thirty years. Convinced of the Bible's teaching about the care of the body, he had made up his mind to quit. But he tried and failed so many times that he reached the conclusion that he couldn't do it. We talked and prayed together about it several times, but apparently to no avail.

One evening I visited Brother Johnson and pleaded with him to try once more. But he felt that it was no use. I asked him to give me the tobacco he had in the house and let me take it away. But he said that the craving for it was so great that he would just be forced to go into town and get some more. He despaired of ever being rid of the habit.

As I sat there and looked at the man and thought back through the preceding months to what he had been and the progress that he had made, I felt impressed that it might be God's will to give him some special help. At my suggestion, we knelt together and presented our problem again to the Lord. Only this time we asked God, if it would be to His glory, to miraculously take away from Mr. Johnson the craving for tobacco.

The next morning the tin of tobacco confronted him. It was the usual time for a smoke, but he left the tobacco untouched and took, instead, some fruit. Quietly and mysteriously the power of God worked, and before the day was over Fred Johnson knew that God had performed the miracle for which we had prayed. From that time on he has never used tobacco in any form and has lost all desire for it.

Mrs. Johnson had gained the victory over the tobacco habit soon after she had begun the study of the Bible but, during a time of discouragement, had gone back to smoking again. Now it was harder than ever to quit. She, like her husband, tried many times but always failed—perhaps after days of agonizing struggle. Her husband was now ready for baptism and she wanted with all of her heart to be baptized with him. But this terrible habit seemed capable of thwarting even her most desperate efforts to throw off its strangle hold on her life.

The struggle went on unceasingly. Mrs. Johnson prayed in her agony of soul until great drops of perspiration broke out on her brow and the tears flowed freely down her face.

With many duties elsewhere in the district, I knew that I could not give Mrs. Johnson the personal help that she needed; so I encouraged her to enlist the aid of a nearby friend. We talked her problem over with Rosy Jacobson, who gladly offered to do all that she could.

Mrs. Johnson did find it a great encouragement to have a neighbor and friend who was sympathetic to her need and upon whom she could call for help at any time. The two visited and studied and prayed together until confidence was built up and the hope for victory looked brighter. Then, one evening after attending the midweek prayer meeting, Mrs. Johnson took the tobacco she had on hand, put it into the fire, and stood there and watched it burn. The ensuing battle was a fierce one, but this time Mrs. Johnson refused to give up in defeat. For three days she engaged in almost continual prayer for strength until, at last, she was assured of victory.

The Johnsons now happily looked forward together to baptism. Now there was nothing that stood between them and their Lord; the world had been left completely behind. There was a joy and a radiance about them that gave witness to everyone that God had performed miracles in their behalf.

An old army buddy of Fred's, Clarence Simmons, met the Johnsons one day. He had heard a little about what had been happening and, when he saw the firm, confident step, the sparkling eyes, and the neat, well-dressed appearance of Fred and his wife, he was truly amazed.

In admiration he said to them, "I don't know what you've got hold of, but, whatever it is, don't ever let it go!"

In fact, the transformation of the Johnsons was the talk of the town. Seventh-day Adventists had been little known in Williams Lake before the Jacobsons and Dan Basaraba had set up their sawmills in the area, and the townfolk quite naturally wondered what these queer people who kept Saturday instead of Sunday were like. But nobody who knew Fred and Elvira Johnson thought that what had happened to them was queer. The result was that several began to inquire with great interest about a religion that had the power to transform lives completely.

During the spring of 1956, John Holstein and I held a series of evangelistic meetings in a rented hall in Williams Lake. The Johnsons rarely missed a meeting even though it meant a ninety-mile drive over rough gravel roads to attend. When we found out that Mr. Johnson had a fine baritone voice, we asked him to sing a solo for the next Sunday-evening service. That night, with the hall well filled with people from the town and the surrounding area, he stepped to the front and clearly sang the beautiful words of F. M. Lehman's hymn, "The Love of God."

As he sang, I felt myself being deeply moved and, wondering if I were the only one so affected, looked about the audience and could see that the Spirit of God was very close to all of us. Before the song was finished, there was hardly a dry eye in the hall.

After the meeting was over that evening, I asked Mr. Johnson what it was that had enabled him to sing with such depth of feeling. He told me that, as he had stepped to the front of the hall, scenes from the past came flooding into his mind. He recalled the times when he had stood in that very same room and had used his voice in ribald songs to entertain his old friends of the world in their drunken dances and parties. In one fleeting moment there came back the memories of the wasted years, of how close he and Elvira had come to breaking up their home; then followed scenes of victory, contentment, and peace. The realization of how much the love of God had done for him overwhelmed his soul and he sang as one who knew from experience what it means to be lifted up by that love from the depths of sin.

By the time the series of meetings in the hall came to an end the warmth of early summer had melted the snow on the hillsides and had broken up the ice on the lake that bordered the town. On a lovely Sabbath morning our people gathered at a quiet little bay along the shore opposite the town and sang together of God's redeeming love as ten precious souls went down into the water for baptism.

The last two were Fred and Elvira Johnson. Their hearts were filled with happiness and they enjoyed to the full this moment that marked their victory in Christ over the world. I baptized Brother Johnson first, and then he stood by and watched while his wife received her baptism. Then together, hand in hand, they walked toward the shore of the lake.

Just before they left the water, they stopped and looked back intently, as though recalling something that no longer existed, and then Fred Johnson turned to his wife and said, "Dear, we've left a lot of sin behind in this lake."